Adventure Guide™ to the
Leeward Islands

Anguilla, St. Martin, St. Barts,
St. Kitts & Nevis, Antigua & Barbuda

Paris Permenter & John Bigley

HUNTER

HUNTER PUBLISHING, INC.
130 Campus Drive
Edison NJ 08818-7816, USA
Tel (732) 225 1900; Fax (732) 417 1744
E-mail: hunterpub@emi.net
Web site: www.hunterpublishing.com

1220 Nicholson Road
Newmarket, Ontario L3Y 7V1, CANADA
Tel (800) 399 6858; Fax (800) 363 2665

ISBN 1-55650-788-7

© 1998 Paris Permenter & John Bigley

Visit Our Web Site!

For complete information about the hundreds of
other travel guides and language courses
offered by Hunter Publishing, visit us online at:
www.hunterpublishing.com

Cover Photo: Leo de Wys
All other photos taken by authors, unless indicated otherwise
Maps by John Cotter Cartography

1   2   3

Acknowledgments

We would like to thank those who helped on the homefront during our many research trips. Our thanks go to Laurie and Tim Kibel, Cliff and Clara Trahan, Sam Bertron and Rebecca Lowe for all their help. As always, special thanks to Mom and Dad for all their help as we hit the road. Thanks to John Cotter for his professional map-making skills.

Thanks also go to our daughter, Lauren Bigley, who lended her assistance with fact-checking.

Our research was also assisted by the many public relations agencies across the country; their hard work made our jobs much easier. We'd like to especially thank for Anguilla: Medhurst and Associates, Deborah Roker, Marilyn Marx, and Miss Ernie Hodge with the Anguilla Tourist Board. In St. Martin/Sint Maarten thanks goes to Mary Jane Kolassa with YPB. In St. Kitts and Nevis we send a thank you to Tim Benford and Tim III of Benford and Associates. In Antigua and Barbuda, we thank Jay Kash with Trombone Associates. Our special thanks also go to the many informative taxi drivers who shared their wealth of knowlege of the islands.

About The Authors

John Bigley and Paris Permenter are professional travel writers and photographers specializing in the Caribbean. The team contribute travel articles and photographs to many top magazines and newspapers.

Paris and John are the authors of *Adventure Guide to the Cayman Islands*, also by Hunter Publishing. The couple have authored *Caribbean for Lovers, Gourmet Getaways: A Taste of North America's Top Resorts, Texas Getaways for Two, Day Trips from San Antonio and Austin, The Alamo City Guide*, and *Texas Barbecue*, named Best Regional Book by the Mid-America Publishers Assoc. The couple are frequent TV and radio talk show guests and have appeared on several travel shows. Both Paris and John are members of the prestigious Society of American Travel Writers (SATW) and the American Society of Journalists and Authors (ASJA). The husband-wife team reside in the Texas Hill Country near Austin.

Contents

Maps

Charts

Anguilla

St. Martin

Sint Maarten

St. Barts

St. Kitts

Nevis

Antigua

Introduction

The Caribbean holds a special place in the hearts of adventure travelers. Although often portrayed as a destination of sun and fun (which it so delightfully can be), these islands present a myriad of outdoor challenges: scuba diving, snorkeling, cycling, hiking, sailing, just about any type of warm-weather sport imaginable.

Some of the region's most special treasures are found in small packages – islands whose petite size belies their many activities.

The Caribbean spans an area that stretches over 2,000 miles east to west and 1,000 miles north to south, starting just off the coast of Florida and arching down to the coast of South America.

This part of the world is blessed with year-round sunshine, with water warmed by Caribbean currents and shores cooled by gentle trade winds. Winter and summer temperatures differ by only about five degrees.

If you look at a map of the Caribbean, you'll see that the islands arch out like a cracking whip, with the largest islands to the west and the small islands to the east, curving on down to South America and ending with a "snap" at the ABC islands: Aruba, Bonaire and Curaçao back to the west. The whole formation of islands is referred to as the Antilles, usually divided into the Greater Antilles and the Lesser Antilles. The Greater Antilles, as the name suggests, are the Caribbean's largest islands: Cuba, Hispaniola (an island shared by the Dominican Republic and Haiti), Jamaica and Puerto Rico. The Lesser Antilles is comprised of all the other islands. The Eastern Caribbean is another way of saying the Lesser Antilles; the Western Caribbean is comprised of the Greater Antilles and the Cayman Islands.

The demarcation line between the placid Caribbean Sea and the tumultuous Atlantic Ocean is a dotted line of islands: the Eastern Caribbean or the Lesser Antilles. This string of small islands lies draped across the sea like a coral necklace. At the northern end of the chain lie the Leeward Islands: Anguilla, St. Martin/Sint Maarten, St. Barts, Saba, Sint Eustatius, St. Kitts, Nevis, Antigua, Barbuda and Montserrat. Below these islands stretch the Windward Islands, heading all the way down to the Southern Caribbean, the home of Aruba, Bonaire, Curaçao, Trinidad and Tobago.

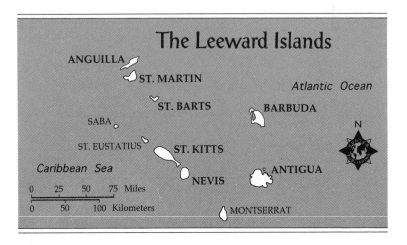

In this guide we've covered the primary destinations in the Leeward Islands in order by their geographic placement north to south. The region is home to three additional destinations, however. These small islands offer vacationers further opportunities for adventure.

SABA: This petite island of just 1,200 residents is part of the Netherlands Antilles, like Sint Maarten, Sint Eustatius, Bonaire and Curaçao. Only five miles square, this rugged isle is a favorite with nature lovers looking for challenging hikes, scuba diving and snorkeling. There are no beaches on this volcanic island. Getting around this island is simple: follow The Road, the only one on the island. The Road leads to The Bottom, the capital of this charming island.

For more information, contact the **Saba Tourist Office** at ☎ 800-SABA-DWI or write PO Box 6322, Boca Raton, FL 33427.

SINT EUSTATIUS: This Dutch island of about 2,200 residents is often known by its nickname, Statia. A quiet hideaway, the focal point of the island is The Quill, an 1,800-foot peak of an extinct volcano. Hikers can climb the steep slopes, verdant with tropical growth, and enjoy a look down into the crater. This rugged island has volcanic sand beaches and waters popular with both snorkelers and scuba divers.

For more information, contact the **Sint Eustatius Tourist Office**, Fort Oranjestraat, Oranjestad, Sint Eustatius, N.A. or ☎ 011-599-3-82433. Additional information can also be obtained from the **Caribbean Tourist Organization**, 20 East 46th St., New York, NY 10017, ☎ 212-682-0435.

MONTSERRAT: Sadly, much of Montserrat is not open to either vacationers or island residents because of volcanic activity. Much of the island has been off-limits for the past two years because of seismic activity and the threat of volcanic eruption; at press time the island was experiencing pyroclastic flows, ash fall and more. Blackburn Airport has been closed to traffic because of its proximity to the danger area. Hopefully, the situation will improve and activity can resume on this beautiful 39.5-square-mile island in the near future.

For more information on Montserrat, contact the **Montserrat Tourist Information Office**, The Huntington Atrium, 775 Park Avenue, Huntington, NY 11743.

When To Go

The time of year you visit the Caribbean may have more to do with your budget than with the weather. Prices can vary as much as 40% between high and low season.

High season generally extends from December 15 through April 15. During this time, prices are at peak and rooms can be difficult to reserve (especially during the Christmas holiday season). Prices soar during Christmas week. After the holidays, package prices (although sometimes not room rates) drop during January. They rise again by February and remain high until mid-April.

Low season covers the summer and early fall months, for two reasons. First, these are the warmest months in the Northeast, the area of the country that often flees to the sunny Caribbean during the chilly winter months, so demand is down. Second, this is hurricane season.

Mention the Caribbean and weather in the same sentence and one concern quickly arises: **hurricanes**. These deadly storms are a threat – officially – from June through November, although the greatest danger is during the later months, basically August through October. (September is usually the worst.)

HURRICANE CATEGORIES

Atlantic hurricanes are ranked by the Saffir-Simpson intensity scale to give an estimate of the potential damage. Category Three and above is considered intense.

Category/Sustained Winds (mph)	Damage
One/74-95	Minimal: Damage primarily to shrubbery, trees & foliage.
Two/96 - 110	Moderate: Extensive damage to shrubs; some trees down. Damage to roofing materials.
Three/111 - 130	Extensive: Large trees down. Some structural damage to buildings. Mobile homes destroyed. Coastal flooding.
Four/131 - 155	Extreme: Shrubs/trees down. Complete small roof failure. Major beach erosion. Evacuation of homes within 500 yards of shore. Hurricane Andrew that smashed into South Florida in 1992 is an example of a catagory four.
Five/155+	Catastrophic: Complete building failures. Small buildings overturned. Low routes inland cut by floods three to five hours before the hurricane's center arrives. Camille, a force five, struck Mississippi & Louisiana in 1969.

Keep in mind, however, that the Caribbean is a large region. We've been in the Western Caribbean when storms were picking up force in the eastern reaches and never felt a gust of wind or saw a wave over ankle-high.

Except for the hurricane season, weather in the Caribbean is a wonderfully monotonous topic.

In the summer, days peak at about 95, with lows in the 70s. In the winter, temperatures run about 5 to 10° cooler. The sea remains warm enough for comfortable swimming year-round.

Special Concerns

Currency

Currency varies by island. Anguilla, St. Kitts, Nevis, Antigua and Barbuda all use the Eastern Caribbean (EC) dollar. Dutch Sint Maarten uses the Netherlands Antilles florin or guilder; French St. Martin accepts the French franc, as does St. Barts. However, you'll find that the American dollar is accepted on almost all islands, although you may receive change in the local currency.

Health

On the smaller islands, medical care can be limited. However, drinking water is safe on all the Leeward Islands and health concerns are at a minimum. No immunizations or special precautions need to be taken, but you do need to have a healthy respect for the damage overexposure to the sun can inflict. For information on specific questions about foreign health concerns, contact the **Centers for Disease Control and Prevention's** international travelers hotline at ☎ 404-3-4559.

Crime

As with domestic US travel, you need to take standard precautions while in the Leeward Islands. Although you may be lulled into a sense of security by the sun and sand, exercise standard, common sense precautions:

- ◆ Do not leave valuables on the beach while swimming. Invest in a waterproof pouch for keys and necessities and lock other items in your car or hotel room.
- ◆ Don't leave valuables unlocked in your rental car.
- ◆ Use hotel safes and safety deposit boxes.
- ◆ Don't walk in isolated areas alone at night.

For information on safe international travel, refer to the Dept. of State's pamphlet *A Safe Trip Abroad*, which provides tips on guarding valuables and protecting personal security while traveling abroad. Write: **Superintendent of Documents**, U.S. Government Printing Office, Washington D.C. 20402.

DID YOU KNOW...

- ◆ The monkey population of the sister islands of St. Kitts and Nevis is two and a half times greater than the human population.
- ◆ Antigua has 365 beaches – one for every day of the year.
- ◆ The island of Saba is the tip of a volcano.
- ◆ The Bath House at Nevis was considered "the most ambitious structure ever erected in the West Indies" when it was built in 1778. Europeans and Americans came to enjoy the 108° waters at the baths, which are still in working order.
- ◆ Anguilla calls itself the "Wreck Diving Capital of the Caribbean." Seven wrecks surround the island and each is upright and accessible to divers of different ability levels.
- ◆ Some residents of Sint Maarten speak Papiamentu, a blend of Dutch, Portuguese, Spanish, English, French and African languages.
- ◆ St. Barts was the only Caribbean island ever ruled by Sweden.

Packing For Adventure

All Visitors:

- ❏ Proof of citizenship
- ❏ Snorkel, fins and mask
- ❏ Sunscreen, aloe vera gel
- ❏ First aid kit
- ❏ Cameras, flash and film
- ❏ Cooler
- ❏ Driver's license for car rental
- ❏ Swimsuit

Divers:

- ❏ "C" card
- ❏ Compass
- ❏ Dive tables and computer
- ❏ Mesh bag and dive boots
- ❏ Dive skin or light wetsuit
- ❏ Dive light and batteries
- ❏ Logbook
- ❏ Emergency medical information
- ❏ Proof of Insurance/ DAN membership card

Bonefish Anglers:

- ❏ Polarized sunglasses
- ❏ Camera to record your catch
- ❏ Wading shoes or boating shoes

Boat-fishing Anglers:

- ❏ Non-skid shoes
- ❏ Camera to record your catch

Hikers:

- ❏ Hiking shoes (broken-in)
- ❏ Extra socks
- ❏ Compass
- ❏ Insect repellent

Sailors:

- ❏ Boating shoes
- ❏ Polarized sunglasses

Introduction

Birders:

- ☐ Binoculars
- ☐ Bird list
- ☐ Bird guide

How To Use This Book

This book is divided into six parts: St. Martin/Sint Maarten, Saint Barthélemy (St. Barts or St. Barth), St. Kitts and Nevis, and Antigua and Barbuda. It covers the Leeward Islands in order – north to south – along the Leeward chain.

The first section on each island takes an overview, looking at what makes that island unique, its history, geography, government, people and culture.

The second section covers travel information you'll need to get to the island and other practical concerns, such as air service, when to go, getting through Customs, cost and island holidays (including festivals). Special concerns – electric currents, currency, health, crime and tipping – are also covered here. Sources of information, including tourist boards that can both help you obtain additional information while planning your trip and assist you while on the island itself, are given here.

The third section for each island covers those items of special interest to the adventure traveler.

After a general look at the island, we'll show you the best way to get around, whether that's by taxi, public transport, rental car, on foot or on bicycle. We'll talk about the island airport, with tips on services found nearby. Car rental companies, found both at the airport and around the island, are included here, along with a general estimate of a day's rental.

Most importantly, this section covers adventures. Adventure is a term for you to define based on your own interests, limitations and abilities. We've offered here a variety of sporting and eco-tourism options both on and off land. Whether adventure travel means wreck diving or birdwatching, you'll find it covered here. For each island, we look at a myriad of different types of adventures for every interest and activity level.

Regardless of the type of activity you choose, know your own limits. Scuba adventures in these islands range from beginners' dives in shallow, placid waters to deep wall and wreck dives. Hikes vary from strolls to sweaty workouts. Water fun spans the spectrum as well, with some choosing to wrestle a fighting bonefish or marlin, while others skip across the sea atop a waverunner or breeze along in a catamaran.

One point to remember, regardless of your chosen activity, is to maintain your fluid levels. At this latitude, temperatures (and humidity levels) soar, draining away precious water and minerals from your body. Replenish often. Carry water on all hikes and boating excursions.

Sun, while being one of the islands' biggest drawing cards, is also a factor to be closely monitored. Wear a hat and a good sunscreen at all times (SPF 15 or higher).

Adventures

On Foot

This section covers walk, hikes and beach strolls on the island. Remember to bring along water for your walks. No matter what the time of year, temperatures can be high and it's important to remain hydrated. If you'll be venturing off the beaten path alone, get last-minute information on possible problems or warnings. It's always a good idea to leave your hiking plan with someone if you're striking out on your own (if you're traveling solo, let the people at your hotel know what you're plans are).

If you're looking for a guided walk, we've included the names and numbers of many operators who specialize in hikes and walks. Most can add a lot to the experience, pointing out unique flora and fauna as well as the area's history along the way. History buffs will find guided walks of the island communities in this section as well. Note that on many of the Leeward Islands (Anguilla, Antigua, Barbuda, St. Kitts and Nevis) driving follows the British tradition on the **left** side of the road, so when crossing streets be sure to look right.

Beach walkers will find plenty of options on all the Leeward Islands but will find especially good choices on Anguilla. Here, long, unbroken beaches offers miles of sand. Another top beach destination is Barbuda, known for its miles of pink sand beaches.

Hikers will find that St. Kitts, Nevis and St. Martin/Sint Maarten present the biggest challenges (especially St. Kitts and Nevis). The rugged terrain of these islands attract many serious hikers.

On Wheels

 Along with scenic drives, we've included cycling tours in this adventure section. Again, remember that on the islands of Anguilla, Antigua, Barbuda, St. Kitts and Nevis driving is on the **left**.

Mountain bikers will find plenty of challenge on St. Martin/Sint Maarten, where organized trips work their way up Pic Paradise. **Casual bikers** will do well on Anguilla, where a flat grade makes for easy pedaling.

On Water

 Watersports, from sailing to windsurfing to sea kayaking, are found throughout the islands. Unique opportunities are found on every island, some which require skill and training, others which can be learned in a simple lesson onshore.

Windsurfers find challenge on several islands. Top competitors sail between St. Kitts and Nevis across a sometimes treacherous channel called The Narrows. For beginners, the calm waters of Nevis' Oualie Beach are favored, as are the waters of St. Martin's Orient Beach.

Scuba diving is an important feature of many vacations in the Leeward Islands. We've covered the special aspects of the island's diving scene, whether that's wreck diving, wall diving or reef diving. Top scuba sites for all abilities, from beginner to advanced, are included, along with a list of scuba operators.

Although scuba diving is found on all the Leeward Islands, the top scuba destinations here are Anguilla (for wrecks), and St. Kitts and Nevis.

This section also covers **snorkeling** destinations throughout the islands.

Surfers and **bodysurfers** can test their skills at several bays in St. Barts.

Fishing is another favorite pastime. Antigua, St. Martin and St. Kitts are well known for their angling opportunities.

Sailors favor St. Martin/Sint Maarten and Antigua for their competitions, charter operations and good conditions. Sint Maarten is home to the one-of-a-kind 12-Metre Challenge, which offers first-time sailors the opportunity to compete on a genuine America's Cup yacht for a few hours.

Sailors prepare for the 12-Metre Challenge on Sint Maarten.

Ferry service is available between Anguilla and St. Martin as well as St. Martin and St. Barts. We'll cover these services in the *On Water* sections for those readers looking for a day trip on a neighboring island.

In the Air

Part of the fun of visiting the Leeward Islands, every one of which offers a view of at least one other island, is **day tripping**. Hop a prop plane and buzz over to a neighboring island for a day of touring. *In the Air* sections point out day trip operators, many which offer complete packages that include lunch, sightseeing tours or rental cars.

Parasailing is also a fun activity for the daredevil set. Look for parasailing operators on St. Martin. And, for a really unique experience, try tandem **skydiving** in Sint Maarten.

On Horseback

 For some travelers, a romp down the beach makes for a perfect afternoon activity. You'll find stables on most islands.

Eco-Travel

 Eco-travel, from birding to rainforest walks to looking for monkeys, is found throughout these islands. **Birders** especially favor Anguilla and Nevis. For rainforest hikes, look to St. Kitts and Nevis, two islands where you can also try your luck spotting wild monkeys in the dense foliage.

Cultural Excursions

 Learn more about the island's unique culture, from its West Indies atmosphere to its historic roots (whether they are French, Spanish, English or Dutch) with a cultural excursion. Special festivals that highlight the culture of the island are included in this section.

Sightseeing

 This catch-all section offers an eclectic collection of things to see and enjoy island-wide. It almost always includes a walking tour of the island's major town, with stops at museums, art galleries, bustling marketplaces and more. Other attractions farther from civilization may include historic forts and plantations, nature preserves and visits to interesting communities.

Introduction

HOW TO SAY...

The Leeward Islands might just contain some of the most difficult-to-pronounce place names in the Caribbean. So you can sound like a local, here's how to say some of the toughest:

Anguilla	an-GWIL-a
Antigua	an-TEE-ga
Barbuda	barb-YOU-da
Nevis	KNEE-vis
Sint Maarten	Saint Martin
Saba	SAY-ba
Statia	STAY-sha

Where to Stay

The *Adventures* section is followed by *Where to Stay*. We've tried to bring a variety of price ranges into this guide. Hotel rates are given according to the following scale (US dollars), based on double occupancy per night in high season:

$	under $150
$$	between $150 and $300
$$$	over $300

Note, however, that prices change quickly, so use these as a gauge and not a set-in-stone figure. Rates also fluctuate greatly by season, soaring to the highest limits from mid-December through mid-April (and hitting a real peak the week between Christmas and New Year's) and dropping to a low during summer and fall months. Call the hotel directly for the best prices and possible packages that may save you money. Types of properties include the following.

Hotels & Resorts

This section covers the island's largest accommodations: sprawling resorts with restaurants, watersports and more.

Condos

Condominium units, popular with those who like the independence of cooking some of their own meals, are found on most of the islands.

Small Inns

Plantation inns, former greathouses that have been converted into bed-and-breakfast operations, are found on St. Kitts and Nevis and offer a unique way to relax and get into the island lifestyle. Other small inns, such as guest houses and properties under 20 rooms, are listed here.

Camping

With its hot climate and primarily privately-owned land, camping is not a common activity in the Caribbean. However, campers will find opportunities on Nevis and Antigua.

Where to Eat

 We've covered an array of dining opportunities in these sections, from fast-food burgers to haute cuisine that will set you back the cost of a day's vacation.

Restaurant prices are given with dollar signs, indicating the price of a meal, drink and gratuity. The dollar signs represent the following prices:

$	under $15 per person
$$	$15 to $30 per person
$$$	over $30 per person

Anguilla

What's Special About It?

Anguilla's beauty is not as flashy as some of the more tropical Caribbean islands that are illuminated with nearly neon displays of flowers. Here, the landscape is flat and fairly featureless, covered with low-growing flora and fauna that fights to take hold in the sandy soil. But that's certainly not to say that Anguilla (pronounced an-GWIL-a) is without beauty.

This tiny island is the king of the Caribbean beach world, a mecca for beach buffs in search of that perfect stretch of sand.

Although only 16 miles from end to end and little more than 35 square miles in all, the island packs in over 30 beaches and numerous nearby cays to tempt sunlovers, snorkelers, sailors, scuba divers and those just looking for a good beach walk or hike. A few beaches bustle with activity, but most are quiet and interruption-free, just pristine boundaries between land and sea.

Anguilla's other beauty comes in the form of her people, perhaps one of the friendliest in the entire Caribbean. Anguillians pride themselves on their hospitality. Local residents greet cars with a wave and exchange "good morning" greetings with those they meet. Crime is rare. If you get lost, just pull over and ask for help. There's a welcoming spirit here that's shared with visitors and instantly makes travelers feel right at home. Expect a quiet atmosphere on this island, no matter when you visit.

This is not the destination of budget charters or cruise ships. It's an island secret that's guarded by a precious few and a treasure protected by a hefty price tag. The island aims for the upper market traveler, who is not shocked by three figure dinner tabs and per-night accommodation rates equal to those found in three- or four-night budget packages on some other islands.

History

Evidence of Anguilla's earliest history is seen in several caves on the island and on nearby cays. Pre-Columbian sites are reminders of Anguilla's earliest inhabitants: the peaceful **Arawak Indians**. These first residents called the island "Malliouhana." Anguilla is one of the richest prehistoric sites in the region and studies are ongoing by archaeologists. The earliest known Amerindian site yielded conch shells broken into drinking vessels as well as axes made from ground shells, flint blades and tools dating to about 1300 B.C. Other sites dating to the fourth century A.D. have also been identified. Archaeologists believe the island then was inhabited by Amerindians, Arawaks of the Saladoid culture. These farmers made settlements at Rendezvous Bay and Sandy Ground by the 6th century.

The Arawaks are credited with carving the Jocahu stalagmite that was found at the Fountain (see *Eco-tourism*, page 46), one of the most important archaeological sites on the island. Jocahu or the "Creator-Giver of Cassava," was probably a spiritual figure that was carved on the cave's stalagmite along with several petroglyphs both at the cave and the freshwater source. Although Columbus came near this island on his 1493 voyage to Guadeloupe, Montserrat, Antigua, St. Martin, St. Croix, Puerto Rico and Hispaniola, no record exists of the explorer sighting flat Anguilla. With a maximum elevation of just 213 feet, Columbus probably sailed right on by, probably without realizing the island existed. European discovery occurred in 1565, most likely by French explorer **Pierre Laudonnaire,** who deemed the island "Anguille" or "eel" for its long, thin shape. (There is some dispute about the nationality of the European discoverer, however, because the word for eel in French, Spanish and Italian is nearly identical.) After European discovery of the island, the Arawak population quickly died off due to disease and enslavement.

Colonization of the island began about a century later when the first English settlers came to Anguilla from St. Kitts, about 70 miles to the southeast. Their attempts were not completely successful, though. By the 1680s, most settlers had abandoned their sugar plantations because of a lack of water and poor soil. Most moved to the British Virgin Islands and St. Croix. Twice the island was attacked by the French. In 1745, a group of 700 Frenchmen were stopped by 150 militia members at Crocus Bay. Forty years later, 400 Frenchmen tried another raid at Rendezvous Bay. The fight worked its way across the island to Sandy Hill Fort. Anguilla sent a boat to St. Kitts and Antigua for help, which came in the form of an English frigate.

Continued development of Anguilla, with its very limited freshwater supply, came slowly. Some settlers tried to grow crops and a small plantation system developed. Fields were worked by West African slaves until 1834 when slavery was abolished throughout the British colonies. The governmental structure of Anguilla changed during the 1600s when Anguilla became part of the Leeward Islands and was administered from Antigua. In 1825, however, the situation altered and Anguilla was united with St. Kitts. By 1871, the island was placed in a federation with St. Kitts, an unpopular move that was protested to Britain. Nevis was later added to the federation but Anguilla was not added until 1951. The relationship between the islands was always a tumultuous one, with claims from Anguilla that St. Kitts ignored the much smaller isle in terms of representation and aid. The ill feelings rose in intensity until a 1967 rebellion brought about **independence** from St. Kitts. The rebellion caught the attention of the world and the tiny island was given the nickname "The Mouse that Roared."

The secession became formal in 1980. Today, Anguilla is happy to exist as a British colony and problems with St. Kitts have long been solved. Anguillians with relatives on St. Kitts will now say that the issues were political, not between the people of the islands.

Geography & Land

Anguilla is the most northerly of the Leeward Islands, located at latitude 18.2 degrees north and longitude 63 degrees west. The island itself is 16 miles long and three miles wide, about 35 square miles in total. Anguilla is also one of the region's driest islands. With no rivers, fresh water is a precious commodity and is now produced by desalination plants. Most buildings feature cisterns and rainwater collection systems. The landscape is dotted with primarily scrub. The highest point on the island is Crocus Hill, rising just 213 feet above sea level. Anguilla's prime asset lies where the land meets the sea. Twelve miles of powdery beaches etch the island's perimeter, creating Anguilla's number one attraction. Thirty-three beaches and caves along with seven islets and cays offer diving, snorkeling and relaxation opportunities.

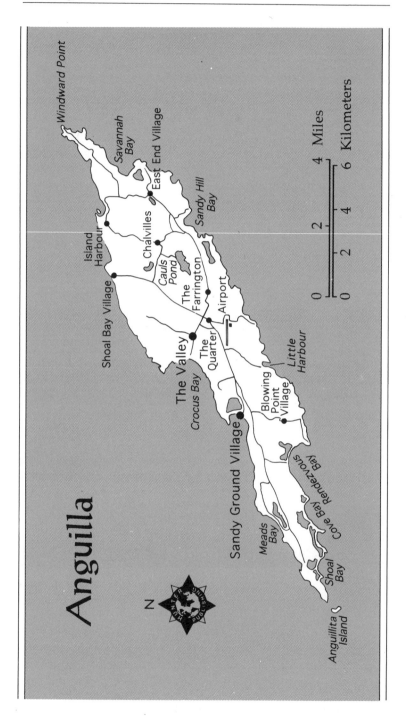

ANGUILLA NATIONAL TRUST

The heritage, both natural and cultural, of Anguilla has been preserved by the Anguilla National Trust. Established in 1993, the trust is charged with several duties, including:

- ◆ Establishing environmental education programs for all Anguillians
- ◆ Promoting and preserving the expression of Anguillian culture
- ◆ Providing advice on matters relating to natural, cultural and historic resources
- ◆ Overseeing the management of all areas designated as National Parks, Protected Areas, Heritage Sites and the National Museum.

The Trust works on projects ranging from monitoring sea turtles to identifying plant species to developing national parks. Walking and hiking trails, an underwater snorkel trail and other sites are maintained by the group.

Several membership categories are available to both residents and anyone interested in Anguilla, from Junior ($5) to Life (US$200) to Supporting (US$500). Family and corporate memberships are also available. Membership includes a monthly newsletter on Trust activities and projects as well as invitations to special events and programs. For information, contact the **Anguilla National Trust**, PO Box 1234, The Valley, Anguilla, BWI, ☎ 264-497-5297; fax 497-5571; e-mail axanat@candw.com.ai.

Climate

Anguilla has a semi-arid climate that's warm year-round. The island receives an average of 35 inches of rainfall annually, much between the months of October and December. The mean monthly temperature is 80°F.

Flora & Fauna

W ith its dry climate, Anguilla doesn't enjoy the lush tropical vegetation of some Caribbean islands. Most natural flora and fauna is low-growing and tolerant of the salty air, strong sun and drought. Look for: beach maho or sea cotton; green agave; aloe vera; organ pipe cactus; buttonwood, a tree that grows in saltwater and brackish water; beach morning glory; cordia, a shade tree with orange blooms; beach or spider lily; *Tabebuia*, the national plant of Anguilla, with pink blooms; calypso oleander; domestic scavola, a dune stabilizer that grows in salt water; giant milkweed, used by locals in past years in the treatment of hypertension; silver buttonwood; pomegranate flower; mahogany tree; natal plum, with star-shaped flowers that smell like gardenias.

At present, Anguilla has no botanical garden or other place to go and see identified plants. The best look at the island's flora and fauna is aboard a weekly **horticultural tour** conducted at Cap Juluca resort at 10:30 a.m. on Friday mornings. Participation is easy; just show up at the front desk and ask to take part in the free tour.

Over 500 species of plants have now been identified as part of the Flora Project by the Anguilla National Trust. This ongoing project has been compiled by a local naturalist and a visiting botanist working to photograph and press plant specimens. Much of Anguilla's vegetation and wildlife was severely damaged by Hurricane Luis in September 1995. However, the island has bounced back remarkably from the devastation remarkably. While trees may be smaller than those of past years, the island is green and dotted with vegetation.

Preservation of the trees following the hurricane has largely been credited to the efforts of the **Anguilla Beautification Club** (ABC). This volunteer group broadcast over Radio Anguilla advising islanders on tree-saving procedures. Before Governor Alan Shave retired, he presented ABC with $3,000. The club has used the money to import trees. It has provided citrus trees for islanders who wished to replace those lost in the storm and has imported shade trees for the island beaches.

EARTH WATCH: *The Anguilla Beautification Club (ABC) continues work to plant trees. One project allows visitors to adopt a tree. The Club also works to beautify the island through tree*

plantings; a current project works at planting trees at the hospital and island schools in a project called "1,000 Trees for the Children." The Club also works to keep the island litter free. Donations can be made to ABC Trees, PO Box 274, Anguilla, BWI.

Birds

The national bird of Anguilla is the **turtle dove** *(Zenaida Aurita)*. Protected by law, the brownish dove can often be seen walking on the ground in search of food. Anguilla is home, both permanently and temporarily, to many other species. Over 120 species are seen on the island; the National Trust reports that 30% of these are globally or regionally threatened or endangered species. Birds often spotted on Anguilla include the green Antillean crested hummingbird, the sugar-loving bananaquit, the frigate bird and the brown pelican.

The mangroves and salt ponds throughout the island provide some of the best habitat for birdwatching. Great blue herons are seen during their winter migration, while permanent residents include the snowy egret, yellow-crowned night heron, lesser yellowlegs or pond dipper, white-cheeked pintail and black-necked stilt.

Iguanas

Iguanas are not native to Anguilla, but following Hurricanes Luis and Marilyn in September 1995, these lizards began to be sighted on the island. They've been identified as a species found only in Guadeloupe and Montserrat; speculation has been made that the iguanas floated over on debris during the storm. To protect and identify the iguana, the National Trust has established a project to learn more about the Iguana iguana.

Sea Turtles

Several species of sea turtle are found in the waters off Anguilla. All are globally threatened or endangered. Hawksbill, loggerhead, leatherback and green sea turtles are found in these waters, but their numbers are not great. Currently, the National Trust is conducting a monitoring program to save these turtles from extinction on the island.

MARINE CONSERVATION

Five Marine Parks are protected under the Marine Parks regulations. The parks are part of a larger project to establish protected areas. It's coordinated by the Caribbean Conservation Association. Funding comes from the Canadian International Development Agency.

Today the marine parks include Dog Island, Prickly Pear and Seal Island Reef System, Little Bay, Sandy Island and the Shoal Bay Island Harbour Reef System. Within these parks, a mooring buoy system has been established. Visiting boats tie up to permanent moorings rather than dropping anchor. These moorings protect the fragile coral reefs and delicate ecosystems. Two types of moorings are found in the parks. Red mooring buoys are for dive vessels only. White moorings buoys are for general use by boats and yachts. All the buoys are marked by location and number and their use is open to all boats 55 feet and under.

To use the moorings, permits are required. The cost of tying up private vessels to a mooring buoy for one day is US$15 (charter vessels pay $22). It is illegal to drop anchor – except with written permission, which is granted only for boats over 55 feet. Boats pay the mooring fee to an officer at the Department of Fisheries and Marine Resources posted at the Marine Base in Road Bay.

EARTH WATCH: *To preserve the delicate coral reefs surrounding Anguilla, marine conservation laws: prevent taking, breaking, walking, standing or anchoring on coral; prohibit jet skiing; prohibit spearfishing; prohibit littering (a fine of up to EC$250 is collected).*

Government & Economy

This **British Crown Colony** is led by a governor and deputy governor, both British and appointed in Britain. Seven elected, one ex-officio and two nominated members, a Speaker and Deputy Speaker, make up the Legislative Assembly. An Executive Council is composed of members of the government, the Governor, the Deputy Governor and the Attorney-General. These ministers have direct responsibility over all matters except those that are directly reserved for the Governor's office and for the legal matters that are the responsibility of the Attorney-General.

Much of the island's economy is dependent upon **tourism**. Anguilla's tourism industry is composed of both day visitors from St. Martin and long-stay visitors.

Other industries include fishing, farming, salt production and boat building. The small island is also an investment and banking center. The island has no taxes on income, capital gains or estates or other taxation on individuals or corporations. Many companies are incorporating in Anguilla to take advantage of the tax-free climate.

Currency

The island's currency is the **Eastern Caribbean (EC) dollar**. As of press time, the rate of exchange was EC $2.70 to US $1. There are no currency exchange controls. US dollars are seen more often than the EC dollar. However, if you do convert money into EC, convert your money back before heading home. Eastern Caribbean currency is not traded on the market and many banks cannot make conversions.

People & Culture

Just under 9,000 residents live on this island, including many transplants from the US as well as Great Britain and Canada. The predominant religion is Anglican, followed closely by Methodist. Seventh-Day Adventists, Baptist and Roman Catholic worshippers are also found here.

Travel Information

When to Go

Any time of year is a good time to visit Anguilla. If you're budget-conscious, low season months (from mid-April through mid-December) are preferable. Look for rates as much as 50% lower during this time. The weather is fairly constant year around, although the threat of hurricanes looms over the area from June through November (the risk is highest in September). Rates are lowest during hurricane season (also the time when temperate weather in the Northeast lowers visitor numbers).

Customs

Admission through Anguillian Customs is quick and easy. Visitors are allowed to bring in items compatible with their intended stay. If you arrive in Anguilla aboard the ferry from St. Martin, you'll pass through Immigration and Customs in Blowing Point. Customs can sometimes be a little slow as many Anguillians return home with their St. Martin purchases, so allow some extra time for this.

Cost

Anguilla is not ashamed to say that it wants to attract the high-end visitor, the vacationer who is not on a budget or looking for bargain packages. Corporate executives, Hollywood types and other well-to-do travelers make up much of the island's elite business. Anguilla, although known for its upscale accommodations, has something for everyone, with 17 properties under $75 per night, 24 under $100 and nearly all guest houses under $50 per night. Also, during special promotions, many of the mid-range hotels offer competitive rates. In the Caribbean, Anguilla's prices compare closest to those seen on Grand Cayman (although accommodation costs on that western island are generally lower.) Closer by, Anguilla's costs compare closely to St. Barts. Don't look for charter flights, budget packages or even two-for-one coupons on this island. Accommodations include an 8% government room tax. There is no sales tax on purchases.

PRICE CHART

Soft drink, restaurant	$2.50
Rum punch	$2 - $5
Hamburger	$10
Gallon of gas	$2.20
One day rental car	$35

Holidays

CALENDAR OF EVENTS

New Year's Day	January 1
Good Friday	Varies; same as in the States.
Easter Monday	Varies; same as in the States.
Labour Day	May 1
Whit Monday	late May
Anguilla Day	May 30
Queen's Birthday	June 16
August Monday	first Monday in August
August Tuesday	follows August Monday
August Wednesday	follows August Tuesday
August Thursday	early August
Constitution Day	August 8
Separation Day	December 19
Christmas Day	December 25
Boxing Day	December 26

Although Anguilla enjoys a festive atmosphere year around, definitely the biggest blowout of the year is **Carnival**. Starting on the first Monday in August and continuing to mid-August, Carnival brings colorful parades, pageants and lots of music to the island. Swimsuit competitions, a bands festival, street dancing, arts and crafts exhibitions and Caribbean night with calypso, soca and reggae artists are scheduled. Carnival also brings boat racing – the island's number one sport.

BOAT RACING

Boat racing is considered the national sport of Anguilla. Races are conducted using sleek vessels, 15 to 28 feet in length. The island-made boats recall the history of Anguilla. Boat racing dates back to the early 1800s when Anguillians, realizing that the low rainfall made sugarcane and other agricultural crops unsuccessful, turned to the sea. Sailors and fishermen worked the waters around the island in boats about 17 to 20 feet in length. Like today's racing boats, these vessels did not have a deck and were powered by a jib and mainsail held by a single 25-foot mast. At the end of a workday, fishermen often raced each other back to shore. The schooners and sloops that provided transportation between Anguilla and other islands also often raced and rivalries grew. By the early 1900s, boat racing wasn't just a way to quicken the commute back to Anguilla, it became a competition.

Fishermen and sailors raced back to Anguilla to take part in competitions such as August Monday, the start of the island's largest festival.

Today, the boats are primarily constructed in Island Harbour on the northwest side of the island. On competition days, Anguillians and visitors line the shores to cheer on the competitors. Three classes of boats are raced. Class A boats, 28 feet long, have a maximum speed of about nine knots and a 12-person crew. Class B boats are 23 feet long, move at seven knots and have a crew of seven. The Class C vessels are 15 feet long, run four to six knots and have a four-person crew.

All the boats are wooden and are built primarily of marine plywood or white pine. A single spar hoists a jib and a mainsail. You'll see the boats, their sleek, shiny hulls reflecting the Caribbean rays, as you drive around the island. Most are kept dry docked in their captain's front yard, proud reminders of the racing sport that binds together Anguillians many times a year.

Races are scheduled on festival days, including: New Year's Day, Easter Monday, Anguilla Day, late May Whit Monday, Queen's Birthday (June 16), and August Monday, Tuesday, Wednesday and Thursday (all in early August). The Heineken Regatta is held in August and the Champion of Champions Race in mid-August. The viewing grounds are typically at Island Harbour or Sandy Ground and at Blowing Point or Meads Bay.

During Carnival, the **Anguilla International Arts Festival** is held for a week to highlight the work of artists from throughout the world. The works entered in the competition must have an Anguillian theme, so artists are expected to spend some time on the island before the competition. Special hotel and airfare rates are available for the international artists. Prizes are US$10,000 for the first place winner and $5,000 for second place and at least four paintings are chosen for reproduction as postage stamps. For more information, contact the Devonish Gallery, PO Box 304, The Valley, Anguilla, BWI (☎ 264-497-2949 or fax 264-497-2735) or the Anguilla Tourist Board, PO Box 1388, The Valley, Anguilla, BWI. Other festivals throughout the year include the following.

- ◆ **National Cultural Education Festival**, in February. This special event celebrates Anguillian culture with traditional dancing, storytelling, games, crafts, local foods, music and plenty of fun. Sponsored by the National Trust.

- ◆ **Moonsplash**, March. This annual concert is held on "The Dune" on Rendezvous Bay.

- ◆ **Earth Day**, April.

- ◆ **World Environment Day**, June. Includes clean-up projects across the island.

- ◆ **Christmas Fair**, December. Held at the Governor's residence, this fair celebrates the holiday season.

Transportation

Flights

Anguilla is served by **Wallblake Airport**, located in the central part of the island near the capital city of The Valley. Word is that the government is currently looking for another site to accommodate the airport, one that will permit an extended runway to accept larger aircraft. Arrival in Anguilla requires a passport for all travelers except Anguillians or Americans who can show a birth certificate and official photo ID or driver's license. Air travelers arrive at Wallblake Airport either by American Eagle from American's hub in San Juan, Puerto Rico or by connection from nearby Sint Maarten (either via plane or ferry). The flight from Sint Maarten takes approximately seven minutes and costs about US $70 round-trip (daylight fare); air charter between the two airports runs $300 per person. For information on air connections, contact: **American Airlines,** ☎ 800-433-7300, (on the island, ☎ 264-497-3131); **WINAIR,** ☎ 264-497-2238 or 264-497-2748, fax 264-497-3351. Each offer daily flights from Sint Maarten. **LIAT** (☎ 800-468-0482, 800-981-8585, 264-497-5000) has daily flights from Antigua, St. Kitts and St. Thomas. **Tyden Air** (☎ 800-842-0261, 264-842-0261 or 264-497-2719, fax 264-497-3079) offers charter service anywhere in the Caribbean and day tours to St. Barts, Nevis and Virgin Gorda, as well as daily flights to St. Maarten. Tyden also offers flights to St. Thomas and St. Kitts. **Air Anguilla** (☎ 264-497-2643) flies to Sint Maarten.

FLYING TIME: Antigua, 1 hour; San Juan, 1 hour; St. Thomas, 45 minutes; St. Kitts, 35 minutes; St. Maarten, 7 minutes.

Departure tax upon leaving the island by plane is US $10 per person.

Ferry Service

Visitors also arrive by ferry from St. Martin. The 20-30 minute ride from Marigot on the French side of St. Martin to Blowing Point, Anguilla costs US$10 each way (plus a US $2 departure fee each way). The ferry allegedly runs every half-hour (on the hour and half-hour), but don't set your watch by it. We arrived at 10:15 for the 10:30 ferry and departed (on a standing-room-only vessel) at 10:50.

Some ferries are extremely speedy but have small capacity; others are roomier but a little slower. It's all luck of the draw as to which vessel will arrive.

To take the ferry to Anguilla, stop by the open-air ferry station on the north end of the market in Marigot. Go up to the window, pay your $2 departure tax and sign up on the manifest sheet, listing your name, passport number and nationality. The ferry fee will be collected on board.

Arrival

Upon arrival in Anguilla by either ferry or plane, you will need to show proof of citizenship. Passports are the easiest way to show citizenship; official photo ID along with a birth certificate with a raised seal can also be shown. A return or onward ticket is also necessary.

By Private Boat

Arrival by private boat means clearing Customs and Immigration in Blowing Point's ferryport or at Road Bay, Sandy Ground (the Customs office is located at the wharf; Immigration is at the Police Station). Note that Anguilla's waters are protected (see *Marine Conservation*, page 24) and fines are levied for dropping anchor without permission.

Special Concerns

Pets

Some pets may be brought to Anguilla. Contact the **Agriculture Department** at ☎ 264-497-2615 or the vet at 264-497-4600/4601 at least six months prior to your visit.

Health

There's no need to worry about the drinking water or food supply in Anguilla. Bottled water is served at most restaurants because the island's drinking water supply is collected rainwater, but tap water is safe to drink. Most resorts have a doctor on call for guest emergencies. The new **Princess Alexandra Hospital** (☎ 264-497-2552) in Stoney Ground just outside The Valley also offers medical care and outpatient services; the emergency room is staffed around the clock.

Dress

Swimsuits are de rigueur on the beach, but wear a cover-up away from the sand and swimming pool. Evenings are typically casually elegant, although jackets are usually not required. Call for dress recommendations if you have questions. Nude and topless sunbathing is prohibited on Anguilla; to soak in a little more sunshine than a bathing suit allows, travel to the clothing-optional beaches on nearby St. Martin.

Crime

One of Anguilla's greatest assets is its low crime rate. With its excellent economic position, crime is rare. However, no destination is completely crime-free. Use the same precautions you would exercise at home.

Drugs

Anguilla exercises strict anti-drug laws. Marijuana is an illegal substance and possession of it can result not only in large fines but also in a prison term.

Business Hours

Most stores are open 8 to 5, Monday through Saturday. Only a few are open on Sunday. The post office is open 8 am to 3:30 p.m.; closed weekends.

Electricity

110 Volts AC.

Money Matters

CURRENCY: Either US or Eastern Caribbean (EC) dollars are accepted. EC and US exchanged at a fixed rate, $1US = EC $2.70.

ATMs in Anguilla are not connected to the international system so vacationers will find that their cards are useless.

TIPPING: Usually added to your bill, but check with individual establishment.

Weddings

To set up a wedding on Anguilla, both parties must show proof of citizenship and a divorce decree, if applicable. A death certificate must also be shown if either party is widowed. All documents must be in English. The cost of the marriage license varies by how long you've been on island. If either one of you have been on Anguilla for at least 15 days before the wedding date, the marriage license is US$40. If your stay has been shorter, the cost is US $284. Two witnesses are necessary. For more information, contact **The Registrar**, Judicial Department, The Valley, Anguilla, BWI, ☎ 264-497-2377/3347.

Communication

TELEPHONE CHARGES: Don't plan to just "reach out and touch someone" from Anguilla – you might as well just bring them along. Long distance calls to the US run about $2.50 per minute. Hotels often levy surcharges on top of this. Also, 800 toll-free numbers will not work from Anguilla. If you need to place a call to an 800 number, dial 400 instead of 800; you will be charged $2 per minute. (To reach 800 numbers at American Airlines, call the local number: 497-3131.)

INTERNET: Cable and Wireless, with an office in The Valley, has Internet service available to visitors. Dial 1-900-468-4638 (HOT-INET) on your modem to connect at a charge of 25¢ per minute. For configuration requirements, call **Cable and Wireless** on the island, ☎ 467-3100 or 467-3648.

MEDIA: Anguilla is home of a daily newspaper (*The Daily Herald*). For a listing of what's happening, look for the free *What We Do in Anguilla*, distributed at area hotels. Three radio stations fill the local airwaves: Radio Anguilla, Caribbean Beacon and ZJF 105.3 FM. Television broadcasting includes Channel 2 and the Network Community Television.

Sources of Information

For more information on Anguilla, contact the **Anguilla Tourist Board** at ☎ 800-553-4939, 264-497-2759, fax 264-497-2710 or write Anguilla Tourist Information Office, P.O. Box 1388, Old Factory Plaza, The Valley, Anguilla, West Indies. Staff members are available from 8 to 5 Atlantic Standard Time (one hour ahead of Eastern Standard Time). While on the island, stop by the Tourist Board in The Valley at Factory Plaza, ☎ 264-497-2759.

Internet users can find a good deal of up-to-date Anguilla information on the following Web sites: http://galaxy.cau.edu/Anguilla and http://www.candw.com.ai/~atbtour.

Out on the Island

This is a relatively small island, so plan to have a look at most of the island during your stay. Getting around is easy – just stay on the main road to zip from end to end – and yet at the same time a little difficult because road signs are practically non-existent. Nonetheless, just about every road feeds off the main road so you can't go too far astray.

The center of the island is home to the capital town (city would be an exaggeration) called The Valley. The community is home to the government offices, the tourist board, the national museum and several good restaurants. Unlike many Caribbean capitals, it is not located on the waterfront but sits near the island's highest point, Crocus Hill. Just south of The Valley is Wallblake Airport, arrival point for many visitors.

South of The Valley runs the main road (yes, everyone calls it "the main road"). It heads southwest of town through the village of George Hill and past the turnoff for Sandy Ground Village, the fishing and boating headquarters for the island. You'll find a good pullover on this stretch from which to look down on the town of Sandy Ground, a veritable strip of sand tucked between the bay and Road Salt Pond, from which islanders produced sea salt until a few years ago.

The main road continues southwest, traveling past a few houses sprinkled among the low-growing vegetation. To the left at a traffic signal not far past the Sandy Ground turnoff lies the turn for Blowing Point, the ferryport that connects the island to nearby St. Martin.

Continuing west, the road reaches the island's top beaches and luxury resorts, the destination of many Anguilla vacationers. This area is also a stop for another kind of Anguilla vacationer – migrating birds. Salt ponds filled with brackish and salt water attract birds to this region. Rendezvous Bay Salt Pond near Sonesta Resort Anguilla, Cove Pond and Gull Pond near Cap Juluca and Meads Bay Pond near Frangipani Beach Club draw many feathered winter visitors as well as a year-round population.

The north end of the island is also home to several good birding ponds. This side of the island has fewer guest accommodations, but is a good destination for the traveler on a budget. Most travelers make the quick trip to this part of the island, however, for a look at its beaches. Follow the main road through The Valley and past Stoney Ground, then take a left at the fork to reach Shoal Bay (you'll see signs advertising beach bars and shops). This is one of the top beaches on the island and the most active beach for sunbathing and a little bar hopping. Other travelers take the right at the fork and continue on the main road to the next main fork, turning left to the community of Island Harbour, where many of the island's boats are constructed. This is also the site of Scilly Cay, a popular afternoon excursion both for lunch and for snorkeling and sunbathing.

From Island Harbour, follow the main road back around to The Valley. It's a quiet, winding drive that takes you past The Copse, the most tree-covered portion of the island.

Anguilla

Getting Around

Rental Cars & Taxi Service

If you plan to travel around the island, by far the most economical transport is a rental car. Taxis are not cheap, so a rental car is preferable for most guests. Public transportation is not available on Anguilla. Taxi service, both in cars and 12-passenger vans, is available throughout the island. All taxis are on a call basis. You can ask for a taxi to be dispatched at the airport or the ferryport in Blowing Rock. We used **Austin's Taxi Service** (☎ 264-497-6660, beeper 2111-239) and can recommend this service for its thorough knowledge of the island.

TAXI RATES

Airport to:

Blowing Point Ferry	$8
Cap Juluca	$18
Casa Nadine	$5
Cove Castles	$20
East End	$11
Island Harbour	$13
Malliouhana Hotel	$14
Shoal Bay Beach	$10
Sonesta Resort Anguilla	$18

Blowing Point Ferry to:

Cap Juluca	$15
Casa Nadine	$11
Cove Castles	$17
East End	$16
Island Harbour	$17
Malliouhana Hotel	$12
Shoal Bay Beach	$15
Sonesta Resort	$15
Taxi within The Valley	$5

Car Rental Companies

Rental car prices vary with operator and model, but a typical mid-size car or a jeep runs about $35 per day. A three-month Anguillian driving permit is required of all drivers. The fee is US $6; this license can be obtained form the rental car companies. Speed limits are maximum 30 mph throughout the island (20 mph in some areas). Tall traffic bumps slow down speeders.

Apex Car Rental	☎ 264-497-2642
Avis Rent a Car	☎ 264-497-6221
Budget Rent a Car	☎ 264-497-2217

C-Breeze Ltd.	☎ 264-497-2133
Caribbean Rentals	☎ 264-497-4135
Concept Car Rentals	☎ 264-497-3661
Connor's Car Rental and Sales	☎ 264-497-6894
Hertz Car Rental	☎ 264-497-2934
Highway Rent a Car	☎ 264-497-2183
Island Car Rentals	☎ 264-497-2723
Romcan Mini Mart and Car Rentals	☎ 264-497-6265
Roy Rogers Car Rentals	☎ 264-497-6290
Summer Set Car Rental	☎ 264-497-5278
TLC Car Rental	☎ 264-497-3290
Thrifty Car Rental	☎ 264-497-2656
Triple "K" Car Rental	☎ 264-497-2934
Uncle Ernie's Car Rental	☎ 264-497-2542

Anguilla

There are no car rental agencies at Wallblake Airport or at Blowing Point ferryport, so most travelers take a taxi to their hotel and call for a rental car from there. (The rental agencies offer free delivery and pick up.) Arrange to meet your agency representative in the hotel lobby to fill out the requisite papers and to obtain your Anguillian driver's license.

Guided Tours

Guided island tours are available from most taxi drivers at a cost of $40 for one or two people, $5 for each additional person. Guided excursions are also available from: **Austin's Taxi Service**, ☎ 264-497-6660; **Bennies Travel & Tours**, ☎ 264-497-2788; **Chandeliers Tours & Shows**, ☎ 264-497-6259; **Malliouhana Travel & Tours**, ☎ 264-497-2431; **Multiscenic Tours**, ☎ 264-497-5810; and **Paradise Ventures Tours & Bus Services**, ☎ 264-497-2107.

At the Airport

Anguilla is served by **Wallblake International Airport,** located just a few minutes from The Valley and a short drive from most resorts. Arrival at the airport is easy; Customs and Immigration is fast and friendly.

You'll find brochures, maps and tourist board information at the airport just as you pass outside the customs area.

Outside the airport terminal taxis are available. Car rental companies are not located at the airport so most people take a taxi to their hotel and phone for car delivery once settled.

The beach at Shoal Bay.

Beaches

Anguilla is deservedly noted for its spectacular beaches, stretches of near-white sand against an aquamarine backdrop. The atmosphere at the various beaches varies from playful to placid. Regardless of which beach you select, the mood is friendly and laid back. A few beach vendors are found on the island's busiest stretch of sand, Shoal Bay, but even here the sales are very low-key and you'll be able to enjoy undisturbed sunbathing all afternoon. All beaches are public.

Here's a look at some of the top beaches on Anguilla:

Shoal Bay. Even if you opt for a quieter stretch of sand, you've got to budget time for a look at this classic beach, one of the best in the Caribbean. Chalk-white sand stretches for two miles and just yards away snorkelers find reefs and even a snorkel trail (see *Adventures, On Water*, page 42). Shoal Bay has the most typical "beach bar" atmosphere in Anguilla, with casual eateries and bars sprinkled along the sand. Beach chairs and umbrellas are rented by the day for a few dollars.

Sandy Ground. This beach, stretching alongside the community of Sandy Ground, is a favorite with boaters, windsurfers, waterskiers and sunbathers. Some of the island's top restaurants are located nearby.

Rendezvous Bay. Largely undeveloped, this beach runs past Sonesta Anguilla and The Dunes Preserve. Take a long stroll on the chalky sand that's occasionally interrupted by rocky shoreline.

Little Bay. This secluded beach is primarily reached by boat and is popular with snorkelers, scuba divers and birders.

Barnes Bay. Located on north side of the west end, this beach is popular with snorkelers and windsurfers.

Maundays Bay. Home of Cap Juluca, this half-moon crescent invites sunbathing (snorkeling is best enjoyed elsewhere).

Cays & Islets

The waters surrounding Anguilla are home to several small cays and islets that are accessible by boat for a day of sunbathing, snorkeling and birdwatching. Check with boat operators for a day trip to the following sites:

Prickly Pear Cays. Good for snorkeling.

Sandy Island. Another popular snorkeling area, Sandy island is located out from Sandy Ground. Stop by the Sandy Island Beach Bar and Restaurant offices next to the Police Station in Sandy Ground between 10 a.m. and 3 p.m. daily for transportation out to the island. The restaurant serves Anguillian lobster as well as fish, chicken and ribs. For information, ☎ 264-497-6395.

Scrub Island. Located just off the eastern end of the island, this site is a popular day trip. One of the larger islets surrounding Anguilla, Scrub Island runs two miles long by one mile wide and includes the ruins of an abandoned resort and even an old dirt airstrip.

Anguillita Island. Located off the southwest shore; uninhabited.

Sombrero Island. Home to many sea birds.

Dog Island. This desert island is home to blue-footed boobies. Visitors can walk the perimeter of the island and enjoy a day with a real Robinson Crusoe feel. Get a boat to drop you here for a full day's excursion; depart from Sandy Ground.

Adventures

On Foot

Caving & Hiking

Several hikes are available for visitors interested in environmental and archaeological sites. **Abideen Cave,** on the far east side of the island, is a good hike. Follow the main road as far as possible, then walk to the light tower. Follow the coast through a big field of Turks Head cacti and frangipani and turn west toward the cave. Dolphins may sometimes be spotted in the channel that divides this far east end from Scrub Island.

Another good hike is to a cave at Katuche Bay. Park by the Governor's residence off the main road in George Hill, cross the road and look for the trailhead. The route leads to **Cavanna Cave**, a site once mined for phosphorus. The trail is well marked and fairly easy. It crosses a former 1800s cotton plantation and is the only closed canopy walk in Anguilla.

On Wheels

Cycling

With its flat grade and light traffic, Anguilla makes a good destination for cyclists. Rentals are available from **Multiscenic Bicycle Rentals** on George Hill Road (☎ 264-497-5810). Motorcycles and scooters are also available for rent on the island. Call C & C Enterprises in Sandy Ground (☎ 264-497-

5196/5954) for information. Scooters are also available through most hotel desks. Scooter rentals run about $35 per day and helmets are required. Drivers must have a $6 permit.

On Water

Scuba Diving

 Anguilla is just making its move into the world of scuba diving and has pristine sites. It offers adventure in the form of coral reef dives as well as wreck dives. Some popular dive sites include:

Sandy Island, 30-70 feet. A good site for sea fans and soft corals.

Sandy Deep, 15-60 feet. A mini-wall offers divers the chance to spot hard corals, abundant fish life and occasionally stingrays.

Aughors Deep, 110 feet. This deep dive includes a look at black coral; large pelagics are often spotted.

Frenchmans Reef, 10-40 feet. Look for schools of reef fish on this cliff-edge boulder. Popular with underwater photographers and beginners.

Prickly Pear, 30-70 feet. An underwater canyon, this site includes ledges and caverns. It is often home of nurse sharks that rest on its sandy bottom.

Grouper Bowl, 25-50 feet. Hard coral formations are found here.

The Coliseum, 25-50 feet. Hard coral formations and schooling fish spotted here.

Sand Canyon, 90 feet. An underwater canyon that comes up to within 25 feet of the surface. A popular dive.

Little Bay, 15-30 feet. Training and night dives often use this site, which is a nursery area for small fish; good underwater photography site.

Wreck Diving

Numerous wrecks lie in the waters off Anguilla. Four were sunk in 1990 as part of an ecological program and all the wrecks are intact and upright on the ocean floor.

> **Wreck of *Ida Maria*,** 60 feet. Deliberately sunk in 1985, this 110-foot freighter is home to many schools of fish; Anguilla's famous lobsters are often spotted here.

> **Wreck of *M.V. Sarah*,** 80 feet. Deliberately sunk in June, 1990, this 230-foot vessel is home to a wide variety of marine life.

> **Wreck of *M.V. Meppel*,** 80 feet. Also sunk in June 1990, the *Meppel* is intact and sits just inside the sail reef system.

> **Wreck of *M.V. Lady Vie*,** 80 feet. Sunk in June 1990, this intact vessel is also located near the sail reef system.

> **Wreck of *M.V. Commerce*,** 45-80 feet. Sitting on a gently sloping bottom, this 1986 wreck has an abundance of fish life and rays are often spotted here.

> **Wreck of *M.V. Oosterdiep*,** 75 feet. Deliberately sunk in June 1990, this upright wreck is home to many fish. Stingray are often spotted here.

Dive Operators

Anguilla has two dive operations, located in Sandy Ground and Island Harbour. **The Dive Shop,** The Valley, ☎ 264-497-2020, fax 264-497-5125, in Sandy Ground, a 5-star PADI international training center; and **Anguillian Divers Ltd.** in Island Harbour, ☎ 264-497-4750, fax 264-497-3723. Rates average about $45 US for a single-tank dive, $80 for a two-tank dive and $55 for a night dive. Divers are charged a $1 per tank Government Marine Park surcharge on all dives.

Snorkeling

Snorkeling is another popular underwater activity around the island. A marked **snorkel trail** is found off Shoal Bay East. Maintained by the National Trust, the site has been mapped and can be easily followed by most snorkelers. (Storms sometimes move the markers, so check with the National Trust before heading out in search of the trail.) Stop by the National Trust office at the National Museum in The Valley or ask your hotel's concierge for a map of this snorkel trail. Laminated for use underwater, the maps are available for a $5 deposit; $4 is returned when the map comes back to the office. To check on the snorkel trail or to obtain a map, call the National Trust at ☎ 264-497-5297.

The snorkel trail offers a diversity of sites that show the marine life and underwater formations found in Anguilla's waters. To reach the snorkel trail, follow the main road down to Shoal Bay. The trail is located just off the point east of Uncle Ernie's. The trail also features sites that illustrate underwater damage, such as that caused by Hurricane Luis, algae invasions and white band disease, a bacterial disease that spread throughout much of the Caribbean in the 1980s. At this site, dead elkhorn coral can be seen. The trail also identifies brain coral, boulder coral and natural defenses used by reef creatures such fire coral, which stings predators (and swimmers!) when touched. There's a turtle habitat area where hawksbill turtles live year-round.

Watersports

Watersports are available from most of the large resorts as well as from beach operators at Shoal Bay. Jet skis are not allowed on Anguilla.

Sailing

Day excursions from Sandy Ground are available on the *Chocolat,* a 35-foot catamaran. From 10 a.m. to 4 p.m., visitors swim and snorkel around Sandy Island and Prickly Pear. Lunch and complimentary drinks are provided. For reservations, ☎ 264-497-3394; cost runs $80 per person. **Sunset cruises** are also available aboard *Chocolat.* Hors d'oeuvres and complimentary drinks are served on the 5-7 p.m. excursion; $50 per person. In Sandy Ground, **Sail Bing** (☎ 264-497-5673/6395) also offers a 37-foot yacht for charter, with a private cabin. The boat is available by the day or week and also for sunset cruises.

Boating Excursions

Charter excursions for a day of snorkeling or for day trips to St. Martin, Nevis, St. Barts or Saba are available from several operators. Charter excursions to a deserted cay or just for a scenic tour around the island are also available. Operators include: **Anguilla Sails**, Sandy Ground (☎ 264-497-4636/2665); **Anguilla Water Sports**, Meads Bay (☎ 264-497-5821); and **Sandy Island Enterprises** at Blowing Point (☎ 264-497-6395/6334) and Sandy Ground (☎ 264-497-5643). Most of these operators offer deep-sea fishing cruises, waterskiing, speed boat rentals, diving, day sails, sunset and moonlight cruises and more.

SCILLY CAY

Just off Island Harbour lies the tiny Scilly Cay, home of the Gorgeous Scilly Cay Restaurant. This private island offers a free boat ride (or a moderate swim if you choose), a lunch restaurant and a day of sunbathing and swimming. Snorkelers (bring your own gear) will find nearby reefs.

In the Air

Island Hopping

Day trip flights to nearby Saba, St. Martin, Statia, Nevis and St. Barts are popular aerial adventures. The flight from Sint Maarten to Anguilla takes approximately seven minutes and costs about US$70 round-trip (daylight fare); air charter between the two airports runs about $300 per person. Flights to the Dutch side of Sint Maarten are available from **WINAIR** (☎ 264-497-2238 or 264-497-2748, fax 264-497-3351) and **Air Anguilla** (☎ 264-497-2643). Day trips to area islands are also available from **LIAT** (☎ 800-468-0482, 800-981-8585), with service to Antigua, St. Kitts and St. Thomas. **Tyden Air** (☎ 800-842-0261, 264-842-0261 or 264-497-2719, fax 264-497-3079), with day tours to St. Barts, Nevis and Virgin Gorda, also makes the longer trips to St. Thomas and St. Kitts. Flightseeing and aerial photography is also available from Tyden Air.

On Horseback

Horseback riding is available through **El Rancho Del Blues,** at Blowing Point. One-hour rides on the beach and in the countryside are offered at 9, 11, 2:30 and 4:30; riding lessons are also available. For more information, ☎ 264-497-6164.

Eco-Travel

Birding

One of the top eco-tourism activities on Anguilla is bird-watching. The Anguilla National Trust has issued the Field Guide to Anguilla's Wetlands, which includes many of the species commonly seen here. The Anguilla Beautification Club has printed a brochure called *Birds of Anguilla and Their Mangrove Habitat*, with additional information on good birding sites.

Mangroves found along the ponds and shorelines protect the soil and also provide a nesting place for many bird species. Four species of mangroves are found on Anguilla (red, white, black and button-wood); many were planted in a 1994 project led by the Anguilla Beautification Club. Residents of these mangrove ponds include the blue heron, snowy egret, yellow-crowned night heron, white-cheeked pintail and black-necked stilt.

Cove Bay Pond and **Gull Pond** near Cap Juluca are two top birding sites on the island. These ponds provide a year-round habitat because, unlike some ponds on the island, they do not dry out between rainy seasons. Across the island, there are 13 permanent saltwater and brackish water ponds.

Cove Bay Pond is a nesting site for the Wilson's plover, snowy plover, black-necked stilts, willet, least terns, royal terns and Wilson's phalarope. A recent survey reported 53 bird species at this pond. Other species sighted included the green-backed heron, spotted sandpiper, lesser yellowlegs, long-billed dowitcher willet, barn swallow, black-throated blue warbler, yellow-throated blue warbler and ring-billed gull.

The Cap Juluca ponds can be enjoyed by any island visitors. Bird guides are available at the hotel.

Archaeological Tours

Anguilla's rich archaeological sites are under exploration. The Anguilla Archaeological and Historical Society has worked since 1981 to preserve and learn more about the island's history. The Society also is working to establish the National Museum in The Valley to contain exhibits on the island's Amerindian history.

To learn more about the efforts of the Society, write the **Anguilla Archaeological and Historical Society**, PO Box 252, Anguilla, BWI.

The Archaeological and Historical Society is working to prepare eco-tours in conjunction with the National Trust. For more information, call the **Tourism Board** while on the island at ☎ 264-497-2759 or from the US at ☎ 800-553-4939.

The National Trust is also working to help in the establishment of the **National Museum**. Currently, the National Trust is housed in the building with the fledging museum.

The Trust is also working to establish several other important eco-tourism sites throughout the island, including:

> **Fountain Cavern National Park**. One of only two such sites in the world, this cavern is home to a carved stalagmite of Jocahu, a spiritual figure. The fountain will be developed as a national park; estimated opening date is January 1999.

> **Big Spring National Park**. Located in Island Harbour, this limestone sinkhole contains 28 petroglyphs. Traced to the Taino Indians around 900 A.D., the petroglyphs are presently being protected until the site can be developed into a national park.

> Plans call for the half-acre site owned by the government and managed by the National Trust to include a botanical trail, nature walk and a viewing platform with benches so that visitors can look into the cavern at the petroglyphs. The site will be open daily sunrise to sunset and admission will be free. For developments on this site, call the National Trust at ☎ 264-497-5297, fax 264-497-5571 or e-mail axanat@candw.com.ai.

> **Underwater Snorkel Trail**. This seasonal attraction is located at Shoal Bay East and will operate during the summer months. The site includes 14 marked attractions and visitors can obtain a laminated underwater map from area hotels or the National Trust's office at the National Museum in The Valley.

> For more information, see *Adventures, On Water*, above.

Cultural Excursions

 Travelers can enjoy a look at the culture of Anguilla through song and dance with a visit to the **Mayoumba Folkloric Theatre**, a group that plays every Thursday night at La Sirena Hotel in Meads Bay. For reservations and information, ☎ 264-497-6827.

ANGUILLA NATIONAL LIBRARY

The Valley is home to the new Anguilla National Library, a Caribbean-style building designed by a local architect. The library includes reference and computer materials for Anguillians and is the home of the island's Heritage Collection. A Saturday morning storytime welcomes young visitors ages five to 10 years old. Visitors can also stop in to view paintings and exhibits by local artists.

The National Library is seeking assistance with the purchase of books, computers, software and audio-visual materials. Contact the **Anguilla Library Service**, The Valley, Anguilla, BWI, ☎ 264-497-2441.

Other Sports

Although it may seem to the visitor that all sports revolve around the water, Anguilla is actually very active in several land-based sporting areas. Cricket is a major passion here, followed by tennis, soccer, basketball, cycling and other activities.

Tennis

Public courts can be found at East End School and Ronald Webster Park in The Valley. Special arrangements may also sometimes be made at the courts of other hotels, consult with the pro.

Golf

Anguilla has no golf courses. For golfing, take the ferry or a commuter flight over to St. Martin.

Soccer

Football or soccer can be viewed at the Ronald Webster Park, north of the post office in The Valley. You'll find a game most weekend afternoons.

Sightseeing

 The pride that Anguillians have in their tiny isle is evident in the large number of museums – albeit primarily small, privately owned ones – found here. Each has a specialty and it's well worth visiting several museums when you're ready to take a break from the beach.

National Museum, The Valley. This project is just in its inception and at press time permanent exhibits were not yet in place. The museum does have a new home, a Caribbean-style building that it currently shares with the National Trust. The collection includes both natural and social history and will soon be displayed at the site. For an update, call the Tourist Board at ☎ 264-497-2759 or the National Trust at ☎ 264-497-5297.

Heritage Collection, Pond Ground, East End, ☎ 264-497-4440. This excellent museum is the work of Colville Petty OBE, an authority on Anguilla's rich history. Housed in part of Petty's home, the museum spans the entire range of the island's history, from its Amerindian days to the 1967 Revolution. The collection includes several zemis, a three-pointed stone that was kept in caves by the Arawaks and worshipped for control of the weather. An Arawak shell necklace, a hollowed conch shell that served as an early vessel and spindle whorls, used to spin cotton to make hammocks and religious symbols for the Arawaks are also on display. Anguilla's more recent history is also in evidence. Spatalashes, fishermen's sandals made from used car tires (kind of a predecessor of the Tyva sandal), eggbeaters made from sea plants and sea fans used as flour sifters testify to the ingenuity of the early residents. Some of the most fascinating exhibits cover the 1967 secession revolution, including a photo of Colville Petty meeting the troops. Anguillian currency, never used, as well as a gun taken from a St. Kitts policeman during the disarming at Wallblake Airport, fill out the collection.

This fascinating museum is open Monday through Saturday, 10 a.m. to 5 p.m. and Sunday by appointment. Talking to Colville Petty about the island's history is well worth the $5 admission charge (children under 12 pay $2).

Sydney's Antique Museum, George Hill, ☎ 264-497- 2135. This museum, located on the north side of the main road in George Hill, takes a look at Anguillian history through exhibits of household artifacts, implements and furnishings. Located in a blue house of traditional Caribbean style, the museum is open 10 to 6 daily.

The Pumphouse Bar, Sandy Ground, ☎ 264-497-5154. Stop by this bar in Sandy Ground, across the street from the dive shop, for a look at the equipment used in the production of sea salt up until a few years ago. The Pumphouse is open 8 p.m. to 2 a.m. and is closed Sundays and Mondays.

Wallblake Historic House, The Valley. This historic site is under restoration. Located across from the tourist office, the Wallblake site dates back to the 18th century. The traditional plantation house was the home of planter Valentine Blake (the v in Valentine was pronounced like a "w," so this soon became Wallblake House.)

Koal Keel, The Valley, ☎ 264-497-5075. Now a notable restaurant, Koal Keel was once called The Warden's Place. Built by slaves, many of whom lived just across the street from the great house, this site originally headed a cotton and sugarcane plantation that spanned the land from The Valley to Crocus Bay. Today, the house is furnished with period antiques and includes a 200-year-old oven still used by the restaurant. Enjoy a look at the historic home, visit the upstairs bakery and then head down to the rum tasting room for a complimentary sip or two!

Where to Stay

 Accommodations add an 8% occupancy tax and a 10% service charge to the bill. For an updated price list, contact the Anguilla Tourist Board and request a copy of the *Anguilla Rate Guide*.

Hotels & Resorts

Sonesta Beach Resort Anguilla, Rendezvous Bay West, ☎ 800-SONESTA, 264-497-6999, fax 264-497-6899. $$$. The Sonesta Anguilla is one of the most memorable resorts in the Caribbean. Styled like something right out of 1001 Arabian Nights, this lavish resort dazzles with mirrored tiles, elaborate mosaics and a unique Moroccan architectural style. It sits perched right on the edge of a three-mile-long beach. One hundred guest rooms include private balconies, marble baths, TVs, mini bars, hair dryers, safes, cool tile floors and a decor that continues the Moroccan theme in cool pastel shades. Oceanfront rooms have spectacular views of the long beach and beyond to the hills of St. Martin. Guest facilities include complimentary use of snorkel gear, sea kayaks, windsurfers and Sunfish, as well as two tennis courts (for day and night play), fitness center, gift shops, children's playground and freshwater pool. Rental bikes are available.

The Sonesta Anguilla is located adjacent to a brackish pond, excellent for morning and evening birdwatching. By Anguilla standards, the Sonesta is one of the best deals on the island. Children 12 and under share a room with parents at no additional charge.

Malliouhana Meads Bay, ☎ 800-835-0796, 264-497-6111, fax 264-497-6011. $$$. This intimate, 56-room hotel is perched on cliffs overlooking a tranquil sea and yet another perfect Anguillian beach. Guest rooms here are private, spread among 25 manicured acres. Complimentary facilities include use of snorkeling and fishing gear, waterskiing, cruises to nearby cays, windsurfing, Sunfish, Prindle catamarans, four tennis courts (three for night play), two pools, Jacuzzis, fitness facilities and a playground.

Cap Juluca, Maunday's Bay, ☎ 888-8JULUCA. $$. Cap Juluca, named for the native Arawak Indian Rainbow God, is an exclusive getaway offering privacy and pampering. The 58 guest rooms and junior suites, seven full suites and six pool villas all have complimentary mini bars, marble baths and hairdryers. Some units feature a kitchen with refrigerator and dining room. Guest facilities include three tennis courts, croquet, beach, pool, Sunfish, kayaks, windsurfing, fitness center, snorkel trips and sunset cruises.

Eco-travelers will find joy in Cap Juluca's *Guide Guide to Birds*, which identifies the many species spotted here. Salt ponds at the entrance to the resort are a favorite site for many birds. Every

Friday at 10:30 a.m. the resident horticulturist offers a guided tour of the resort's many native plant species.

The picture-perfect Maunday's Bay, Cap Juluca.

EARTH WATCH: *Cap Juluca was recently a runner-up for the Green Hotelier of the Year award from the Caribbean Hotel Industry Conference. The resort is noted for its extensive use of native plant material, an on-site nursery for plant propagation, use of reclaimed water for irrigation, composting, installation of an herb/vegetable garden, use of biodegradable bags for landscape refuse removal, use of fluorescent lighting for landscape and security lights, implementation of energy-saving suggestions in guest and public areas, use of non-polluting freon for refrigerator and air-conditioning units, use of biological predator insects for pest control and use of eco-friendly cleaning products, can recycling programs and emphasis on the environment. Eighty percent of the plants on the 180-acre resort are native varieties and, with the nursery on property, the resort grows most of its own materials. Some potential future projects now being researched at the property include*

> *water-saving devices in toilets, solar hot water*
> *heating, solar lighting and expanded use of*
> *fluorescent lighting.*

Cove Castles, Shoal Bay West, ☎ 800-223-1108 or 310-440-4225; local number 264-497-6801. $$$. This villa resort caters to the guest looking for privacy, peace and quiet. These stark white two- and three-bedroom getaways have a contemporary exterior and a tropical decor inside. Complimentary amenities include snorkeling, Sunfish sailboats, sea kayaks, bicycles, tennis, video players and library, concierge service, cable TV and a personal housekeeper. Also available at additional charge are deep-sea fishing, sailing excursions, tennis instruction, massage and more.

Birders will find a nearby salt pond and good opportunities to observe seasonal migrations. Special weeks are marketed to birders.

Small Inns

Casa Nadine, The Valley, ☎ 264-497-2358. $. This little guest house makes it possible to do Anguilla on a tight budget. Rooms are $20 per night and there are definitely no frills. The inn is within walking distance to everything in The Valley, however. Weekly rates are offered.

Pond Dipper, Sandy Ground, ☎ 264-497-2315. $. For birders this economy property is conveniently located next to a pond; it is also within walking distance of the beach. It's nothing fancy, but it is situated on a quiet residential street. Rooms have ceiling fans and maid service. Weekly rates are available.

Where to Eat

 Look for a 10% to 15% service charge on your bill in most establishments, although some of the smaller restaurants and bars such as The Dunes Preserve leave the tip at your discretion. Check with your waiter if you can't tell if the service charge has already been added to your total.

Beach Bars

LeBeach Bar and Restaurant, Shoal Bay, ☎ 264-497-5598. $$. This casual, open-air eatery is just steps from the action of Shoal Bay. Choose from sandwiches, burgers, chicken salad, lobster salad and rib platters. The staff here is helpful and friendly and the food is tasty. Open for breakfast, lunch and dinner.

Uncle Ernie's, Shoal Bay, ☎ 264-497-3907. $. One of Anguilla's best-priced eateries, this popular beach bar serves up barbecue chicken, burgers and crayfish in a relaxed atmosphere. Wrap a towel around your waist and come straight in from the beach.

Madeariman Reef, Shoal Bay, ☎ 264-497-3833. $-$$. Watch the busiest beach on the island from this beach bar, which offers table service and dining in a cool, shady environment. Burgers and pizzas are available or enjoy dishes with a more local flair. Seafood kabob, conch fritters or lobster fettucine elevate this restaurant to more than the typical beach bar.

The Dunes Preserve.

The Dunes Preserve, Main Road east of Sonesta, no phone. $-$$. This charming bar and restaurant, set up high above the seashore, is one of the Caribbean's hidden gems. Constructed entirely of recycled ship parts and driftwood, this open-air roost gives visitors the feeling they're visiting Robinson Crusoe. In actuality, they're visiting the restaurant and bar of Bankie Banx, Anguilla's best-known musician. The friendly reggae singer performs on Friday nights and during lunch on weekends and other times you'll find him bartending. Go for a drink and to enjoy the view, then stay for dinner. Besides its title as the island's funkiest bar, this is also one of Anguilla's best restaurants (and that's saying something on an island favored by gourmands). Don't miss this one.

Caribbean

Old House Restaurant, George Hill. $$-$$$. Anguillian dishes are the specialty in this historic home. Choose from curried dishes, grilled steaks and fresh seafood. Breakfast, lunch and dinner daily.

Continental

Casablanca, Sonesta Anguilla, ☎ 264-497-6999. $$$. This open-air restaurant has a casually elegant atmosphere. Offerings include Anguilla crayfish, black angus tenderloin, shellfish pepper pot and several pasta dishes. Dinner is served from 6 p.m. to 10 p.m. nightly, except Monday and Thursday. (Children under 12 years should dine between 6 p.m. and 7 p.m.; after that time the restaurant encourages a quieter atmosphere for adults only.)

Chatterton's on the Beach, Cap Juluca. $$-$$$. This casual open-air restaurant features island specialties such as black bean soup, island fish soup, lobster sandwiches and sautéed shrimp.

Eclipse At Pimms, Cap Juluca, ☎ 264-497-6666/6779. $$$. Fine dining is part of the experience at Cap Juluca. Eclipse at Pimms, the main restaurant, serves up California-Provençal cuisine using local, fresh fish and produce. Executive chef and partner of Eclipse at Pimms is Serge Falesitch, also executive chef and partner of the Eclipse restaurant in West Hollywood, CA. Formerly executive chef at Spago's, Falesitch and partner Bernard Erpicum, formerly of Ma Maison, bring to Anguilla a unique cooking style and notable cuisine. Specialties include grilled peppered ahi tuna with artichoke, sun-dried tomato and olive vinaigrette, baby snapper with tomato, black olive, fennel and basil vinaigrette and wild rice and white corn risotto with grilled quail.

Koal Keel, The Valley, ☎ 264-497-5075. $$$. One of the Caribbean's finest restaurants, Koal Keel is an attraction and a fine restaurant rolled in one. The menu includes island pea soup, a purée of pigeon peas and Caribbean sweet potatoes, and Calalloo soup. Your evening will continue with entrées such as coconut shrimp, "Drunken Hen" (a Cornish hen baked and blazed with 151 Bacardi) and crayfish grille. The wine list here is a veritable book; the restaurant has its own wine cellar with separate climate-controlled rooms for red and white wines. You'll make all the dining decisions at once, including dessert selections, which are made to order. Vanilla crème brûlée, mango tarte soufflé and mango sorbet make the perfect end to a meal. After you've eaten enjoy a walk around this historic site followed by a complimentary rum tasting.

Gorgeous Scilly Cay, Island Harbour, ☎ 264-497-5123. $$-$$$. This offshore restaurant features Anguillian lobster as well as grilled fish, chicken and ribs. Just walk up to the dock in Island Harbour and wave; a boat will come over to transport you to Scilly Cay. Visitors can also enjoy a swim or a snorkel around the reefs and there is live music on Wednesdays, Fridays and Sundays. The restaurant is open for lunch only, 11 to 5 p.m., Tuesday through Sunday.

Anguilla

Shopping

Most serious shoppers head to St. Martin on a day trip, but Anguilla does tempt shoppers with one good opportunity: art. This tiny island is home to numerous artists, both Anguillian and relocated from around the globe, who work in oils, wood and other mediums. One of the best known is Cheddie Richardson, a self-taught carver who sells his work at **Cheddie's Carving Studio** on the main road in The Cove (near the Sonesta turnoff). Working in mahogany, walnut and especially driftwood, the artist portrays birds, dolphins, fish and humans.

Other artists on Anguilla include Lucia Butler (specializing in wooden house plaques), Marj Morani (scenes of island life and hand-thrown pottery), Jo-Anne Saunders (sculpture, fabric, murals), Susan Graff (island scenes), Tanya Clark (Japanese woodblock prints) and Courtney Devonish (sculpture and pottery). For more information on Anguilla artwork, contact the Tourist Board in The Valley.

Nightlife

 Well, nightlife is, to put it mildly, pretty darn quiet in Anguilla. This island has a lot of things, but a hopping night scene is not one of them. For nightlife, plan to spend a night over on St. Martin for some casino action, dancing and shows. For most Anguilla visitors, nightlife means a gourmet meal enjoyed at a luxurious pace, perhaps followed by an after dinner liqueur or a moonlit walk. Some beach bars and restaurants do offer evening entertainment, however. Here are a few places where you'll find evening fun.

The Dunes Preserve, Rendezvous Bay. No phone. Reggae musician Bankie Banx plays on Friday nights and during full moons.

Johnno's Beach Stop, Sandy Ground, ☎ 264-497-2728. From Wednesday through Sunday nights, this hopping beach spot offers live performances, usually starting about 8 or 9 p.m. (4 p.m. on Sundays).

La Sirena Hotel, Meads Bay, ☎ 264-497-6827. On Monday nights, this hotel offers the sounds of a steel drum band at 7:30. Thursday nights mark the Mayoumba Folkloric Theatre at 7:30 p.m., featuring traditional songs and costumes.

Gorgeous Scilly Cay, off Island Harbour, ☎ 264-497-5123. Wednesday, Friday and Sundays live music is offered at this offshore cay.

St. Martin/Sint Maarten

What's Special About It?

This island calls itself "a little bit European and a lot Caribbean." It's a fitting description of a most unusual political situation: two nations sharing a single, small piece of land. The smallest mass on the globe shared by two nations, it's a peaceful neighboring of French and Dutch that offers vacationers twice the cultural experience. Travelers can enjoy fine French food, topless French beaches, Dutch architecture and Dutch casinos that ring with baccarat and roulette, all in an atmosphere that's definitely West Indian.

Located 150 miles southeast of Puerto Rico, this 37-square-mile island is occupied by Dutch Sint Maarten (pronounced the same as the French side, Saint Martin) and French St. Martin. Since 1648, the Dutch have occupied the southern reaches of the island while the French have claimed the northern side. The demarcation is marked by a simple obelisk between Union Road and Bellevue. Travel is effortless between the two nations, like crossing a county line back in the States. No passports. No Customs. No Immigration. Although the border is almost superficial, there are distinctions between the two countries. Mention "St. Martin" and many visitors will immediately think of topless bathing that's de rigueur on the Gallic beaches. And on one 1½-mile stretch, au naturel is the order of the day. On this portion of the island, the atmosphere is definitely French, with plenty of bakeries to enjoy a baguette or crêpes. French is heard in the markets and there's no mistaking that this is *la partie française*.

The urbanized side of the island is found on its Dutch acres. Most visitors arrive in Simpson Bay's Princess Juliana International Airport. Don't let the modest size of the terminal fool you – this is one of the Caribbean's busiest airports, with direct service from New York, Newark, Miami, Baltimore and San Juan, not to mention Paris and Amsterdam. Regional air service to many small islands also travels through this hub. All those visitors mean plenty of hotel rooms and many are found along Simpson Bay. Each side of the island brims with 4,000 rooms (compared to just 200 on the Dutch side 20 years ago). However, the island was severely hit by Hurricane Luis in September of 1995, requiring the rebuilding of many properties. For some hotels, the storm brought renovations, so many that today the Sint Maarten Hotel and Tourism Association boasts that the island shows a new face, brought on by millions of dollars in refurbishments, many of which were planned for the distant future until Mother Nature forced a speed-up.

The Dutch influence is felt far less strongly in Sint Maarten than the Gallic influence in St. Martin. Although the official language taught in the schools, Dutch is rarely heard on the street. And although it falls under the government of the Netherlands Antilles and the Kingdom of the Netherlands, the US dollar reigns here. The atmosphere is strictly West Indian with an eye toward American commerce. US dollars are accepted freely and shopping on the Dutch side is more American-style than in St. Martin, where goods are more European in style.

Simpson Bay hops with vacationers who come to enjoy pristine beaches, the island's best snorkeling at Mullet Bay and the only golf course on the island. But in nearby Philipsburg it's shopping that draws visitors. Duty-free shops line the busy streets and pedestrians can spend an entire day popping from store to store in this commercial center. Cameras, electronic goods, perfumes and fine jewelry are especially good buys. During the night hours, the Dutch side hops with activity in its glitzy casinos and rocking nightclubs. For the adventure traveler, this island is especially attractive for its boating. Simpson Bay has long been considered a "hurricane hole" and yachts from around the Caribbean come to seek cover in this protected waterway during threatening storms. In any weather conditions, however, Simpson Bay is home to fine vessels and vacationers who have been saving their pennies can charter one for a once-in-a-lifetime cruise to any islands they chart. Or, if you'd rather take the helm, learn to sail from many operators on this side of the island. And, for a taste of competition, sign up for the 12-Metre Challenge, a chance to race aboard an America's Cup yacht for a few hours.

Hikers will also find that this island is a treasure. Covered in verdant, rolling hills that look down on powdery beaches and bird-lined salt ponds, the island offers treks from the easiest to the most rigorous.

History

Once the home of **Arawak Indians** from South America, this island was first called "Sualouiga" or "Land of Salt." Today, visitors can easily see why the Indians chose this name: salt ponds and brackish water are seen throughout the island, especially on its southern reaches. Philipsburg is tucked between the bay and the Great Salt Pond. But it wasn't that salt water that attracted the Arawaks. They were looking for fresh water and found it in fresh-water springs around Paradise Peak, Mount William, Billy Folly and in the lowlands. Artifacts found at these and other sites are preserved in the St. Martin Museum (see *Sightseeing, St. Martin*). Later the Arawaks lost their hold on the island, overthrown by the fierce, cannibalistic Carib Indians for whom the region is named.

The island was spotted on November 11 by **Columbus** during his second voyage in 1493. It was the day of the feast of St. Martin of Tours, a Spanish holy man of the sixth century. And so the island was named, although Columbus did not set foot on the island.

As Spain took little interest in St. Martin, the Netherlands began to consider it as a strategic post halfway between their colonies in Pernambuco, Brazil and Nieue Amsterdam (New York). By 1631, the Dutch began to occupy the island and soon constructed Fort Amsterdam. The new residents took salt from the island's ponds and shipped it back to Holland – a move that didn't go over well with the Spanish. In 1633 the Dutch were tossed off the Spanish-claimed isle and Old Spanish Fort was erected at Point Blanche.

But the Dutch didn't leave for good. From nearby Sint Eustatius they continually attempted to recapture the island. On March 20, 1644, Peter Stuyvesant, later the governor of Nieue Amsterdam, commanded the Dutch fleet in an attempt to control the island. A stray Spanish cannonball shattered his leg, which had to be amputated. But luck was on the Dutch side, and when the Eighty Years' War between Spain and the Netherlands ended, the Spanish no longer needed a Caribbean base and just sailed away in 1648.

Once the island was free, the Dutch at Sint Eustatius sent Captain Martin Thomas to take possession of the island – only to find that the French were already there. A skirmish followed and finally a settlement was reached on March 23, 1648, dividing the beautiful island between the two nations. No one knows exactly how the triangular island was split, but the popular legend is that a French-man and a Dutchman walked in opposite directions around the

St. Martin/Sint Maarten

perimeter of the island with the understanding that the points where they met would be the new border. One tale says the Frenchman took water and the Dutchman beer, causing him to get sleepy and cover less ground. The R-rated version of the fable claims that the Frenchman enticed a young maid to divert the Dutchman for a few hours, helping the Frenchman claim 21 square miles to the Dutchman's 16. However the island was originally divided, its boundaries shifted some 16 times in the coming years before they were settled. Philipsburg became the capital of Dutch St. Maarten and Marigot the capital of French St. Martin.

Soon **slavery** was introduced to the island as the Europeans began to cultivate sugarcane. Slavery was abolished by the French in 1848, although Holland did not emancipate its slaves until 15 years later. The result was the Freedom Path from the Dutch side north to the French, one that ran through a heavily wooded trench up across the border. Until recently, this Freedom Path was still visible and while walking through the thick underbrush it was easy to picture the plight of the runaway slaves as they made their way north to freedom. Unfortunately, much of this important piece of heritage has now been lost with the land cleared for road improvements.

After **emancipation**, the island's agricultural economy worsened. It remained poor until 1939 when it received status as a duty-free port. In 1943 Princess Juliana Int'l Airport opened on the Dutch side and just four years later the island's first hotel began welcoming guests. By the 1950s, Sint Maarten enjoyed a rising tourism industry. Not until the 1970s did the French side follow suit.

TIMELINE

1493 Columbus sights and names the island.
1631 Kingdom of Netherlands occupies island.
1633 Spain recaptures island.
1644 Peter Stuyvesant fights to capture the island
      for Holland.
1648 Spain retreats; French and Dutch move in.
      Dutch/French Treaty of Concordia.
1848 Slavery abolished on French side.
1863 Slavery abolished on Dutch side.
1943 First airport constructed on island.

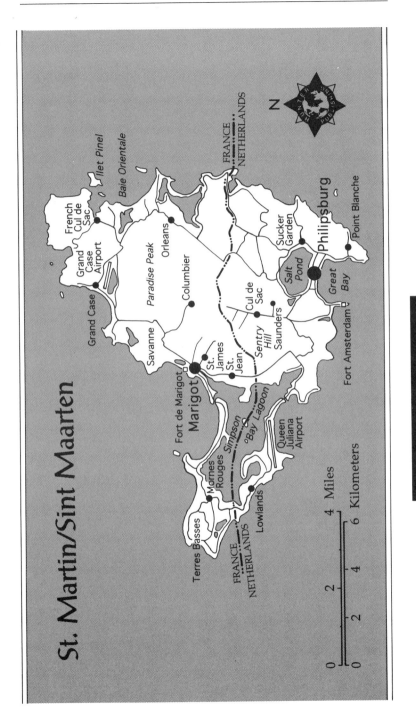

St. Martin/Sint Maarten

Geography & Land

St. Martin is located at 18.5 degrees north and 63.5 degrees west. The island is primarily volcanic, with steep hills and a rugged terrain.

Climate

Temperatures are tropical year-round on this island. The average temperature during the winter season is 80°F. Summer months are warmer and more humid. The average annual rainfall is 45 inches.

Flora & Fauna

Not a lush island, the hills of St. Martin vary in shade from a beautiful green to a parched brown, depending on how recently the last rain fell. Most of the island is covered with low-growing vegetation which can withstand the drier months. Cacti are often spotted alongside scrub. Around the resort areas, look for tropical blooms such as hibiscus and bougainvillea.

Like others in the Leeward chain, St. Martin has imported mongooses, brought to kill the rat population but effective only on the snakes. The island is rich with bird life, however, especially around the salt ponds found on its southern reaches.

Government & Economy

Today, St. Martin belongs to the préfecture of Guadeloupe and is considered to be just another part of France. Islanders are entitled to vote in French elections. The Dutch side belongs to the Netherlands Antilles, part of the Kingdom of Holland. The capital of the Netherlands Antilles is located on the southern Caribbean island of Curaçao.

People & Culture

Over 32,000 people live on Dutch St. Maarten and 28,000 on St. Martin. The island is home to 77 different nationalities, including French, Dutch, Haitian, Dominican, Jamaican, American and Canadian. English is the most commonly heard language, although French is the official language on the northern side of the island and Dutch on the southern. Spanish is often heard here as well.

Travel Information

When to Go

This is a good destination year-round. Keep in mind that prices are highest during peak months (mid-December through mid-April) and reach an all-time high the week between Christmas and New Year's. During Carnival weeks, air transportation to the islands can occasionally be pretty well booked as visitors and former residents come in to enjoy the festivities.

Customs

Because Sint Maarten is a duty free port, there are no restrictions on the amount of goods you can have upon arrival.

Upon return, US citizens can bring back $600 worth of goods (family members traveling together can pool their exemptions). The duty-free allowance on liquor for US citizens age 21 and over is one quart.

St. Martin/Sint Maarten

Holidays

The biggest event on each side of the island is Carnival. On the Dutch side, Carnival occurs after Easter and continues until April 30, the birthday of Queen Beatrix of the Netherlands. The festival includes traditional Caribbean jump-ups, parades and gatherings filled with island dishes and music. The Grand Carnival Parade is the festival's biggest event, a colorful scene with elaborate costumes and a contagious spirit of fun. And for early risers (or real night owls) there's the Jouvert (jou-vay) Morning Jump-Up Parade. This festivity starts at 4 in the morning and continues until sunrise. Carnival's end is marked with the burning of King Momo, a straw figure who "rules" carnival. When King Momo is burned, legend says that the island is left pure.

On the French side, Carnival is scheduled just before Shrove Tuesday, ending on Ash Wednesday.

CALENDAR OF EVENTS

◆ *January*

New Year's Day. Public holiday (both sides)
Pelican Run, Dutch side.
Evian Mountain Bike Race, Dutch side.
Pepsi Cup Optimist Regatta, Dutch side.
La Fête des Rois (Epiphany). A day of feasting and dancing includes the old French custom of serving a cake called *galette des rois*. French side.

◆ *February*

Mid- to late February. Dutch side: **Carnival** with floats, music and Carnival Queen. French side: Carnival with parades, election of Carnival queen. Expect business to stop for about five days.
Beach Cat Regatta, Dutch side.
Pepsi Cup Optimist Regatta, Dutch side.
Mi-Carême (Mid-Lent): Red and black street parade on St. Martin. The red symbolizes the carnival spirit and the black symbolizes the mourning for the Lenten season. French side.

Mardi Gras (Shrove Tuesday). Height of Carnival, dances in Marigot and Grand Case. French side.
Ash Wednesday. Final day of Carnival. French side.

◆ *March*

Heineken Regatta. Both sides.
St.Martin/St. Maarten Anglers Annual Big Fish-ing Tournament. Both sides.
Beach Cat Regatta. Dutch side.
Heineken Regatta. Dutch side.
Pepsi Cup Optimist Regatta. Dutch side.
Anniversary of Treaty of Concordia. (March 23rd).

◆ *April*

Early History Day. Display of historical documents with tour guides and photo competition. French side.
Carnival. Dutch side.
Queen's Birthday. Dutch side.

◆ *May*

May 1, **Labor Day**. Both sides.
May 25, **Ascension Day**. Public Holiday both sides.

◆ *June*

International Blue Marlin Fishing Tournament. French side.
Father's Day Regatta. Dutch side.
Guavaberry Off-Shore Regatta. Dutch side.

◆ *July*

Calypso Music Festival. French side.
July 14, **Bastille Day**. French side.
July 21, **Schoelcher Day**. Celebration of 1848 emancipation day in honor of Victor Schoelcher, the French parliamentarian who led the campaign against slavery. Boat races at Grand Case using Anguillian sailing boats, mini-marathon, bike race ending in Grand Case. French side.

St. Martin/Sint Maarten

◆ *August*
Assumption Day. Both sides.

◆ *October*
October 21, **Antillean Day**. Dutch side.

◆ *November*
November 1, **All Saints Day**. All cemeteries are illuminated with candles. French side.
St. Maarten Day. Dutch side
November 11, **Concordia Day**. Joint celebration with ceremony at Border Monument obelisk commemorating the long-standing peaceful coexistence of both countries on the island. Includes "Around the Island" race, based on historic folk tale about how the island's border was established.

◆ *December*
December 25, **Christmas Day**. Both sides.
December 26, **Boxing Day**. Both sides.
December 31, **Réveillon de Saint Sylvestre**. New Year's Eve celebration with noisemakers and dancing. French side.

Transportation

Entry Requirements

Entry requirements into St. Martin/Sint Maarten are simple. US citizens entering for three months or less need to show either a passport or a certified birth certificate with a photo ID. Canadian citizens entering for 14 days or less must show a passport, birth certificate or naturalization certificate. Canadian vacationers staying over 14 days but less than 30 days will be issued a certificate of admission. Visitors also must show an onward or return ticket. Citizens of other countries should check with their travel agent or the tourist bureau for admission requirements.

Air Service

Air service is available at two airports on the island: **Princess Juliana International Airport** on Dutch St. Maarten and **L'Espérance Airport** in Grand Case on the French side. The French airport is served only by a few commuter flights from St. Barts and Guadeloupe so most travelers arrive in Dutch Sint Maarten.

FLYING TIME: Travel time to the island is 2½ hours from Miami, 3½ from New York, 4½ from Dallas, 5 from Montreal and 8 hours from Paris.

Princess Juliana is a major airport and a Caribbean hub for inter-island travel. **Air France** (☎ 800-237-2747) offers flights from Amsterdam, Brussels, Copenhagen, Frankfurt, London, Milan, Paris, Rome, Zurich and, within the Caribbean, from Guadeloupe and Martinique.

American Airlines (☎ 800-624-6262 or 800-433-7300). Daily service from Miami, New York and San Juan. **ALM** (☎ 800-327-7230). Service from Aruba, Bonaire and Curaçao. **Continental** (☎ 800-231-0856). Service from Newark. **KLM** (☎ 800-374-7747). Service from Amsterdam, Barcelona, Bombay, Frankfurt, London, Lyon, Manchester, Milan, Paris and Rome. **USAirways** (☎ 800-622-1015) flies from Baltimore and Charlotte. **Northwest Airlines** (☎ 800-447-4747) has flights in the high season. **Air Liberte** (☎ 011-590-93-08-58) and **Nouvelle Frontieres** (☎ 011-590-87-27-79) offer flights from Paris.

Inter-island carriers include: **Air Guadeloupe** (☎ 011-599-55-36-51); **Air Martinique** (☎ 011-596-60-00-23); **Air St. Barthélemy** (☎ 011-599-55-36-51); **LIAT** (☎ 800-468-0482, 800-981-8585), with service from Anguilla, Antigua, Puerto Rico, St. Croix, St. Kitts, St. Thomas and Tortola, BVI; **BWIA**, (☎ 800-538-2942, 800-327-7401), with service from Antigua, Barbados, Jamaica and Trinidad. **Tyden Air** (☎ 800-842-0261) offers flights to Anguilla several times daily. **Winair** (☎ 800-634-4907) has service from St. Thomas, St. Kitts, Saba, Statia, St. Barts, Anguilla, Dominica and Tortola.

Charter service is a popular and relatively inexpensive means to get to the islands and is available from these charter companies:

Apple Vacations: departures from Chicago, JFK and Atlanta during high season. ☎ 800-365-2775.

MLT Vacations: departures from Detroit and Minneapolis during high season. ☎ 800-727-1111.

TNT Vacations: departures from Boston during high season. ☎ 617-471-8900.

GWV International: departures from Boston during high season. ☎ 617-449-5460.

Air Canada: departures from Toronto during high season. ☎ 800-422-6232.

Air Transat: departures from Toronto and Montreal. ☎ 514-987-1660.

Alba Tours: departures from Toronto during high season. ☎ 416-746-2488.

Conquest: departures from Toronto during high season. ☎ 416-665-6811.

Signature Tours: departures from Toronto and Montreal during high season. ☎ 416-967-8481.

Sunquest: departures from Toronto during high season. ☎ 416-485-1700.

DEPARTURE TAX: A $12 tax is imposed upon departure from the Princess Juliana International Airport. A 15-franc departure tax is included in the price of airfare for those leaving from L'Espérance Airport.

Cruise Terminal

In Philipsburg, Sint Maarten, the new $2.5 million **Captain Hodge Wharf,** can accommodate up to 600 passengers an hour (triple the size of the former tender pier). It's the first step in a $60 million master improvement plan for the area.

The new wharf includes a Tourist Information Center and is now the disembarkation point for over 650,000 cruise ship passengers annually. The site is named for Captain Arsene Hodge who, beginning in 1938, operated the first government ship delivering mail, passengers and goods between St. Maarten and Saba, Statia and St. Kitts.

The new wharf regularly welcomes cruise passengers from Carnival, Costa, Norway, Cunard, Club Med, Celebrity and other lines.

In Marigot, the cruise pier is located at the market and is used to tender cruise passengers to this area. It sports a new look, thanks to renovations that occurred during the filming of the movie *Speed 2: Cruise Control.*

Special Concerns

Currency

The official currency of Dutch Sint Maarten is the Netherlands Antilles florin or guilder (NAF). On the French side, the official currency is the French franc (FF).

Don't worry about exchange rates or looking for a currency exchange – US dollars are the common means of exchange. Most prices are marked in US dollars and change is given in American greenbacks.

Telephones

International phone calls are *expensive* from both the Dutch and the French sides of the island. Expect a bill of about $40 for even the briefest call back home.

Electricity

The French side uses 220 AC, 60 cycles and all appliances made in the US and Canada will require French plug converters and transformers. The Dutch side uses 110 AC. Most hotels offer both voltages and different plug configurations, but bring converters to be safe.

Health

Water is safe to drink on both sides of the island, although bottled water is often served in restaurants.

Doctors are on call at most island hotels and you'll find several pharmacies around the island (on the French side these are marked with a large green cross). Both Marigot and Philipsburg have hospitals with English-speaking doctors.

St. Martin/Sint Maarten

Crime

With its rising population, crime has become an increasing problem in St. Martin. Exercise the same precautions as you would take at home. Don't leave valuables on the beach while you swim.

Weddings

Dutch Sint Maarten recently changed its marriage regulations, permitting non-resident couples to exchange vows on the island. (For more than a century, non-resident marriages were prohibited.) Today, couples over 21 years of age must make a written request to the Lieutenant Governor to first obtain a temporary tourist permit not to exceed three months. The couples must also submit birth certificates, divorce papers (if applicable) and valid return or onward tickets.

All of these documents must be translated into Dutch by an official sworn translator or a notary public. The request should be mailed to the Lieutenant Governor, Government Administration Building, Clem Labega's Square, Pondfill, Philipsburg, Sint Maarten, Netherlands Antilles. After approval by the Lieutenant Governor, there is a 10-day waiting period and a fee of 90 guilders or about US $50.

On French St. Martin, marriage licenses are available after one partner has resided on the island for a 30-day period. Proof of citizenship, single status and, if applicable, of divorce are necessary. All documents must be translated into French. Both partners must show a medical certificate, including a blood test issued within three months of the marriage date.

Tourist Information

Dutch Side

Call ☎ 800 STMAARTEN for information on the Dutch side of the island, including transportation, accommodations and activities. Alternatively, write to:

St. Maarten Tourist Bureau
Walter Nisbeth Road, 23
Philipsburg, St. Maarten
Netherlands Antilles
☎ 011-5995-22337; fax 011-5995-22734

St. Maarten Tourist Office
675 Third Avenue, Suite 1806
New York, NY 10017
☎ 212-953-2084 or 800-STMAARTEN
Fax 212-953-2145

While on island, you'll find an information center at the cruise
terminal in Philipsburg. Check out the Dutch Sint Maarten Web
site at this address: http://www.st-maarten.com.

French Side

For brochures, maps or information about French St. Martin, call
"France On Call" at ☎ 900-990-0040. This is a toll call and provides
information on all lands which are part of France. You can also
write the tourist office nearest you:

French Government Tourist Office
444 Madison Avenue
New York, NY 10022

French Government Tourist Office
9454 Wilshire Blvd., Suite 715
Beverly Hills, CA 90212

French Government Tourist Office
676 N. Michigan Ave., Suite 3360
Chicago, IL 60611

French Government Tourist Office
1981 Ave. McGill College, 490
Montreal, Quebec, Canada H3A 2W9

French Government Tourist Office
30 St. Patrick St., Suite 700
Toronto, Ontario, Canada M5T 3A3

St. Martin/Sint Maarten

While on island, stop by the St. Martin Tourist Office near the waterfront in Marigot; the office is open Monday through Friday 8:30 to 1, 2:30-5:30 and Saturday from 8 to noon.

Helpful free publications include *Discover St. Martin* (in French and English) and *Reflets*, published by the St. Martin Tourist Office. Another helpful free book is *Ti Gourmet*, an annual guide to island restaurants in French and English. All are available at the tourist office and from many hotels.

Check out the French St. Martin Web site at this address: http://www.interknowledge.com/st-martin.

French St. Martin

Out on the Island

The French occupy the northern region of the island, a rugged land with steep peaks, the island's highest point, verdant farmland, beautiful beaches and quaint villages.

The atmosphere of the French side is somewhat more relaxed than that of its Dutch neighbor. More land on this side of the island and a slower growth rate has, so far, prevented serious overcrowding, though there has been much development in recent years.

The capital of French St. Martin is **Marigot** (pronounced mari-go), a charming community that is a distinct blend of French and Caribbean. The tricolor of France flies here, seen alongside the distinctive West Indian gingerbread architecture. The town meanders along a waterfront that serves as a ferry landing for excursions to and from Anguilla and a cruise ship tender pier used to bring in vacationers for the day. A lively market creates a festive atmosphere. Just steps away, high dollar goods compete for the tourist dollar in sleek, European-style shops.

North of Marigot, the road turns inland and works its way north. Turnoffs take travelers to **Colombier**, the lushest part of the island and **Paradise Peak** (Pic Paradis), the island's highest summit. Both are good excursions for nature lovers and hikers.

Continuing north, the road leads to the town of **Grand Case** (pronounced grand cos), the island's culinary capital. Small gourmet restaurants line the waterfront of this fishing village. The beach at Grand Case is a favorite spot for watching boat races on the island's many holidays.

From Grand Case, travelers can cut across the island to its eastern shores, the home of the island's most popular beach at **Orient Bay**. Lively and dotted with watersports operators and beach bars, this stretch of sand also includes a clothing-optional area.

Getting Around

Rental Cars & Taxi Service

Taxis are one of the best ways to get around the island, especially for the first-time visitor. Steep, winding roads combined with plentiful traffic can be challenging the first day or two, so consider a taxi for the first part of your stay. Taxis travel freely to both parts of the island.

If you'll be traveling extensively during your stay, however, a rental car can be a good investment. Taxi rates from end to end of the island quickly surpass rental rates. Here's a sample of taxi rates around the island:

TAXI RATES

Princess Juliana Int'l Airport to:

Marigot	$8
Grand Case	$20
Nettlé Bay	$15
Orient Bay	$20
Grand Case to Philipsburg	$16

Marigot to:

Grand Case	$10
Philipsburg	$8
Mont Vernon	$15
Orient Bay	$15
La Samanna	$12
Meridien L'Habitation	$18

Taxi rates are set by the government. The minimum rate is $4 for one or two persons; an extra $2 is charged for each additional passenger. The cost rises after 10 p.m. (25% higher) and again after midnight (50% above daytime rates). Taxi stations are located beside the courthouse in Philipsburg on the Dutch side and near the dock in Marigot on the French side. Tips of 10-15% are customary.

Public Buses

Public buses offer an inexpensive and colorful (although not fast) way to travel the island. They run from Marigot to Philipsburg, with other routes to Mullet Bay, Simpson Bay, Cole Bay and Grand Case. Fare ranges from 85¢ to $2. Check with your hotel desk for times. Buses run from about 6 a.m. to midnight and can be flagged down anywhere. They leave every hour from Grand Case.

TRANSPORTATION TO ORIENT BEACH

When a cruise ship is in port in Philipsburg, you can often find cheap transportation to Orient Beach. Look for taxi drivers holding an Orient Beach sign; vans shuttle back and forth for just $5 per person.

Car Rental Companies

Car rentals are available from $27 to $80 per day and a valid driver's license is needed, along with a major credit card (or a major cash deposit). Driving is on the right side of the road. These companies offer rentals on the French side (international code, 011, plus the country code, 590, must be dialed if calling from the US):

Avis, Marigot	☎ 87-50-60, fax 87-97-66
Chreas and Love, Marigot	☎ 87-78-54
Continental, Cripple Gate	☎ 87-77-64, 87-80-81
Dan's Car Rental, Cul de Sac	☎ 87-38-22
Espérance, Marigot	☎ 87-51-09
Flamboyant Car Rental, Grand Case	☎ 87-50-99
Hertz, Galisbay, Marigot	☎ 87-73-01
Hibiscus Car Rental, Nettlé Bay	☎ 87-74-53
Island Trans Car Rental, Saint-James	☎ 87-91-32
Locaraibes, Marigot	☎ 87-81-12
Roy Rogers Car Rental, Grand Case	☎ 87-54-48
Sanaco Car Rental, Grand Case Airport	☎ 87-14-93
Sandy G Car Rental, Sandy Ground	☎ 87-88-25
Sens Unique, Concordia	☎ 87-22-88
Sunny Island, Saint-James	☎ 87-80-21
Tropical Car Rental, Marigot	☎ 87-94-81

St. Martin/Sint Maarten

Scooters & Motorcycles

Scooters are available for about $22 per day (motorcycles from $35 per day and even up to $100 a day for a Harley Davidson). However, realize that traffic can be bad and road conditions, with steep hills and plenty of bumps, will be difficult. Consider this option only if you are a very experienced rider.

Eugene's, Marigot   ☎ 87-13-97, fax 87-08-47
Rent a Scoot, Nettlé Bay   ☎ 87-20-59

Guided Tours

The Ste. Transport Touristique de St. Martin (☎ 011-590-87-56-20) provides a bus to and from Juliana Airport to the French side and offers guided tours.

Sightseeing trips by taxi cost about $30-35 for one or two passengers and about $10 for each additional passenger. Allow 2½ hours for the guided tour and make arrangements ahead of time with the taxi company.

Beaches

 There's no denying that St. Martin's beautiful beaches, nearly 40 in all, are one of this island's top assets. Whether you're looking for pulsating action or blissful privacy, you'll find it somewhere on the island. On the French side, topless sunbathing is standard and nudity is permitted on the nude beach at Orient Bay.

VISITING A NUDE BEACH

Both St. Martin and Antigua are home to clothing-optional beaches, located at Orient Beach and Hawksbill, respectively. Although the atmosphere varies greatly along these two stretches of sand, from boisterous and crowded at Orient Beach to quiet and secluded at Hawksbill, the etiquette remains the same.

- ◆ Don't take photos. Cameras are actually prohibited at Orient Beach and security will come have a little talk with you if you violate this rule.
- ◆ Feel free to join in or not. Clothed, topless and nude vacationers all frequent the nude beach. Stretch out your towel or (at Orient Beach) rent a chaise lounger and soak up the sun in as much or little swimsuit as you choose.
- ◆ Don't assume this is some sort of love-in. Sexual activity is one adventure that's a definite no-no. In fact, families are commonly seen on Orient Beach, both nude and clothed.

Top Beaches

Long Bay (Baie Longue). As its name suggests, this is the largest beach in St. Martin. From here you can walk west to Plum Bay, a shadier stretch of sand.

Grand Case Bay. Located right in downtown Grand Case, this beach is relaxed and a good place to cool off after a midday meal.

Little Cayes. One of the most isolated, this beach can be reached only by boat or by a 30-minute walk from Cul de Sac along a coastal trail.

Galion Beach. These protected waters make them a favorite with beginning windsurfers and snorkelers.

Baie Rouge. Swimmers find good conditions at this quiet hideaway.

Coconut Grove. Families and snorkelers enjoy placid waters at this shady beach.

Baie de l'Embouchure. Protected by a coral reef, these waters are good for sailing and windsurfing.

Baie Lucas. Good diving from a shady beach here.

St. Martin/Sint Maarten

Orient Beach.

Orient Bay. This is the liveliest place on the entire island, definitely the spot to see and be seen. This long stretch of powdery sand is lined with beach bars, restaurants and watersports operators. Chaise loungers and umbrellas are offered for rent all along the beach. The nudist area is on the east side in front of Club Orient; photography is prohibited there.

Adventures

On Foot

The quaint village of **Colombier** is located between Marigot and Grand Case. The lushest spot on the island, this inland settlement is rich with tropical flora, including mango, coconut and palms. Save time for a walk through this traditional Creole village.

Hiking

St. Martin has 40 kilometers of trails of varying difficulties. The most cited hike is the walk between **Paradise Peak** (Pic Paradis), at 1,391 feet the highest point on the island, and **Concordia**. From these heights, hikers enjoy a look at the island from observation decks. Less strenuous but offering a good view is the walk up the stairs to the restored **Fort St. Louis** for a panoramic view of Marigot.

On Wheels

Mountain Biking

Mountain bikers find plenty of challenge on the French side. Especially ambitious cyclists may make the trek (and then buzz down) **Paradise Peak** (Pic Paradis). Another popular route is from **French Quarter to Oyster Pond**, a coastal road where you'll be treated to cool trade winds as well as views of St. Barts. **Colombier**, a scenic village lush with foliage, makes another good tour.

Guided Tours & Rentals

Frog Legs Cyclery (☎ 011-590-87-05-11), at the Howell Center in Marigot, offers rentals as well as guided bicycle tours.

On Water

Scuba Diving

Most scuba diving is done from boats at some distance off shore, where divers are rewarded with good visibility. Reef, wreck, night, cave and drift dives are available. Some top dive sites include **Ilet Pinel**, a shallow dive on the island's northeast coast near Orient Bay; **Green Key**, a barrier reef also near Orient Bay; and **Flat Island** (or Ile Tintamarre), known for its quiet coves and sub-sea geological faults. **Anse Marcel**, on the north side of the island, is another popular choice.

Dive operations also take visitors to the wreck of the *Proselyte* on the Dutch side and to Anguilla. Costs average $45-$65 per dive.

Dive Operators

Dive operators include: **Lou Scuba Club**, Nettlé Bay (☎ 011-590-87-16-61, fax 011-590-87-92-11) is PADI affiliated; **Blue Ocean**, Nettlé Bay (☎ 011-590-87-89-73); **Octoplus**, Grand Case (☎ 011-590-87-20-62); **Orient Beach Watersports** (☎ 011-590-87-40-75); **S.M.C. Dive Center** (☎ 011-590-87-48-61).

Snorkeling

Good snorkeling is found at many locations. Orient Bay, Green Key, Ilet Pinel and Flat Island (Tintamarre) are protected as regional underwater nature reserves or Réserve Sous-Marine Régionale.

Island Ferries

Explore neighboring St. Barts with a quick trip aboard the *Voyager* 2, which departs from Marigot to Gustavia, St. Barts at 9 a.m. and 5:45 p.m. daily (reservations required for Sunday departure). The 1½-hour trip aboard the high-speed boat is comfortable, air-conditioned and includes a stocked bar. The round-trip is $50 plus $9 tax. A package including lunch and an island tour is $80 plus $9 tax and, considering the dining prices on St. Barts, is a real bargain. Car rental costs about $40. For reservations and information, call Corine or Philip at ☎ 011-590-87-20-28 or fax 011-590-87-20-78.

Cruising

For some, adventure on water might include a nude cruise, which travels from the island's clothing-optional beach at Club Orient to Flat Island and the small cays off St. Martin. Full day cruises aboard

the *Tiko-Tiko* catamaran include an open bar, lunch, snorkel gear, umbrellas and floats. Additional trips include excursions to Scrub Island, Anguilla and St. Barts (although trips to Scrub Island and Anguilla are not clothing-optional while on the islands). Cost is $80 per person. *Tiko-Tiko* also does an overnight stay on the island of your choice; the package includes three meals, open bar and berth at $225 per person (minimum four persons). For information, call **Papagayo Watersports** at Club Orient, ☎ 011-590-87-33-85, fax 011-590-87-33-76.

*A catamaran cruise can make
a great day off-island.*

Cruises are also available from **Compagnie des Goelettes** (☎ 011-590-87-10-16, fax 011-590-87-10-19), based in Marigot. They have a 32-meter sailboat offering cruises to Anguilla, Tintamarre and Pinel Island, including lunch buffet. **Seahawk Cruises** (☎ 011-590-87-59-49) offer excursions on a 77-foot catamaran to Anguilla, Prickly Pear or Sandy Island for $70 (plus $6 port tax). The package includes lunch, open bar and snorkel gear. It departs from Marigot Harbor at 9 a.m., returning at 5 p.m.

Yacht Charters

Yacht charters are another popular option. Contact these operators for bareboat or crewed charters:

The Moorings, Oyster Pond, ☎ 800-535-7289; **Sun Yacht Charters**, Oyster Pond, ☎ 800-772-3500; **Stardust Marine**, Port Lonvilliers, Anse Marcel, ☎ 800-634-8822; **Nautor's Swan Charters**, Port Lonvilliers, ☎ 800-356-7926; **Marine Time**, Marigot, ☎ 011-590-87-20-28, fax 87-20-78.

Boaters looking for moorings on the island find plenty of good, anchorages near services and facilities. Some of the more popular anchorages are: **Baie Rouge**, with an anchorage on the east end of the beach; **Nettlé Bay** near Marigot; **Marigot Bay**, good for shopping nearby (Port la Royale Marina located at Marigot); **Friar's Bay**, known for its calm, quiet waters; **Happy Bay**; **Grand Case Bay**, with shops and restaurants; **Anse Marcel**, a protected spot with seclusion and home of Port Lonvilliers, a marina for up to 100 boats with grocery, ship chandlery and facilities; **Flat Island** (Tintamarre); **Orient Bay**, known for its nudist beach; **Oyster Pond**, for good dining and a large marina.

Deep-Sea Fishing

Dolphin, kingfish, sailfish, blue marlin, tuna and wahoo lure deep-sea anglers to these waters. Charters are available by the hour, half-day, full day and by the week, supplying tackle, bait and drinks (and, occasionally, a light lunch). Half-day charters run about $450, full days about $800. For more on deep-sea charters, contact **Sailfish Caraibes** at Port Lonvilliers (☎ 011-590-87-59-71). This operator has a fleet of boats equipped with Fenwick rods, Penn international reels and other top deep-sea fishing gear.

The Sailfish Caraibes Club organizes the **Marlin Open de St. Martin** at Port Lonvilliers. This invitational tournament is con-

St. Martin/Sint Maarten

ducted under IGFA rules and offers $50,000 in prizes. For more information, ☎ 011-590-87-26-58 or fax 011-590-87-02-91.

Water Taxis

Papagayo Watersports at Club Orient, ☎ 011-590-87-33-85, fax 011-590-87-33-76, also offers water taxis from Orient Beach to nearby Pinel and Green Key for $10 and $15 respectively. Pinel Island is especially popular with birdwatchers.

Jet Skiing

Watersports operators line busy Orient Beach. Rent a jet ski and jump the waves for about $50 a half-hour.

Windsurfing

Windsurfing is another popular option and lessons average about $25-30 per hour. Some operators offering windsurfing lessons are **Blue Ocean** at Nettlé Bay (☎ 011-590-87-89-73) and **Orient Watersports** at Orient Bay (☎ 011-590-87-40-75). Friar's Bay, located next to the mouth of Guichard Pond, is a well-protected beach. For information on windsurfing races, contact the **St. Martin Windsurfing Association**, based in Marigot (☎ 011-590-87-93-24).

In the Air

Helicopter Touring

From Anse Marcel, take a helicopter tour to St. Barts or Anguilla aboard *Ecureuil*. Cost is $120 for an Anguilla trip, $180 for St. Barts (per person, four-person minimum). Lunch and island tours are also offered. For details, contact Chantel or Edouard at ☎ 011-590-87-21-87.

Parasailing

Enjoy a bird's-eye view of Orient Beach for about $50 a ride. You'll take off just yards from the sand and it's quite a show, especially on weekends.

Day Trips

From Grand Case, **St. Barth Commuter** offers day trips to nearby St. Barts. Flights depart on Wednesdays at 9 a.m. and return at 4:30 p.m. Round-trip air fare, including taxes, is US $80. A minimum of six participants, maximum of nine, is required. Bookings are accepted only until the preceding Monday at 3 p.m. Additional flights are available to Anguilla, Antigua, Barbuda, Guadeloupe, Nevis, St. Kitts and Statia. For information, contact St. Barth Commuter, Aeroport de Grand Case, ☎ and fax 011-590-87-75-70.

Parasailing at Orient Beach

On Horseback

Bayside Riding Club (☎ 011-590-873664, fax 011-590-873376 or contact your hotel activity desk) offers beach rides, riding lessons, pony rides and even horse leasing. Beach rides follow the surf and, if you're on the island at the right time, full moon rides can be a unique experience. Two-hour rides depart at 9 a.m. and 2 p.m. Private one-hour rides are also offered, along with champagne beach rides. Bayside Riding Club is next to Orient Bay on the road to Le Galion Beach.

Caid and Isa (☎ 011-590-87-32-79) at Anse Marcel (near Le Meridien) offers two rides daily at 9 a.m. and 3 p.m., except on Sunday. Six paso finos are stabled and available for hire at $40 for a 2½-hour excursion that goes over the hills of Anse Marcel to the beach of Petites Cayes, also known as Anse de la Pomme d'Adam or Adam's Apple Cove.

Eco-Travel

Commission for Ecotourism

Two important projects are under the supervision of the French St. Martin's Commission for Ecotourism. Pointe de Bluff, between Baie Longue and Baie Nettlé on the northwest coast, is being preserved. This site is home to **"David's Hole"** or, as it's sometimes known, the Devil's Hole, an unusual sea cave. The second project is at **Oyster Pond** on the east coast where preservation of the green sand beach is underway.

Sightseeing

Once a sleepy fishing village, today **Marigot** is the capital of tourism on the French side. The promenade is lined with expensive duty-free shops, French restaurants, an open-air market and a cruise ship pier. The town is an excellent pedestrian destination and you can walk from end to end, stopping at the bistros and bakeries for a croissant, shopping for French perfumes or just enjoying the West Indian architecture.

Vendor in Marigot's lively market.

Fort St. Louis. Perched over Marigot Bay, this fort is the largest historic monument on the island. It was built in 1767 to protect Marigot and was occupied for a while by the Dutch. Today the fort can be seen from the market in Marigot. For the best views of the city and the western side of the island, take a hike to the summit.

Marigot Market. Located on the docks in Marigot, this open-air market takes place every Wednesday and Saturday. It's a good chance to experience a slice of local life as residents shop for fresh fish and fruit as well as spices. The market continues up to the ferry area, where vendors sell items daily from kiosks aimed at the tourist market: woodcarvings, Haitian paintings, batik pareos, jewelry and more.

St. Martin Museum, "On The Trail Of The Arawaks." This museum is located in the city's southern reaches and is dedicated to preserving the history and culture of St. Martin. Exhibits include a reproduction of a 1,500-year-old burial mound, colonial displays and more. The museum is open Monday through Saturday, 9-1 and 3-7. Admission is $4.

Butterfly Farm (☎ 011-590-873121). This "ferme des papillons" is a unique attraction and well worth the drive. You'll enter the butterfly's world and stroll among plants in which they make their home. The colorful insects are free-flying, gracefully floating and flitting from plant to plant as they eat. Eighty species of butterflies are found here, including many longwings and flames. These tropical species reproduce throughout the year, so you can see the butterflies in different life stages.

Tours are offered at the Butterfly Farm.

The most famous butterfly in the world, the morpho, is seen floating like blue crèpe paper. Its blue tint was once used to make watermarks for US bills. Bring along your camera for this tour. The farm is open from 9 to 4:30; guided tours are $10. Your ticket is valid for unlimited visits to the farm during your stay.

Grand Case. This city (pronounced "grand cos") is the capital of the island's cuisine. No more than a fishing village, the town is nevertheless well known for its fine French restaurants.

Paradise Peak. Pic Paradis is the highest point on the island, soaring to 1,400 feet. A challenge to hikers and mountain bikers, the summit holds two observation decks and offers beautiful views.

St. Martin/Sint Maarten

Where to Stay

There's no shortage of places to stay on the French side of the island. Luxury resorts are extremely popular, and frequently offer villas, rather than rooms.

Hotels & Resorts

La Samanna, ☎ 212-575-7030, 011-590-87-51-22; fax 011-590-87-87-86. $$$. This 80-room resort is often cited as one of the Caribbean's most luxurious. A member of Orient Express Hotels, this complex features rooms with cool white interiors, bamboo and mahogany furniture and a genteel atmosphere. La Samanna was closed by damage from Hurricane Luis, but has reopened with a fresh face and restored grounds.

Club Orient Resort, ☎ 011-590-87-33-85; fax 011-590-87-33-76. $$-$$$. Located on the nude end of Orient Beach, Club Orient Resort is a naturist or nudist resort known throughout the world. Everything – from watersports to dinner – is available for guests to enjoy sans clothes. Just a look at the signs at the beach bar ("No tan lines, no problem") confirms the philosophy of this resort.

Cabins here are modest, camp-like structures with baths and fully equipped kitchens. Guests can stock up with supplies at a small store located on property or take their meals at Papagallo's restaurant located right on the beach. The restaurant and bar are clothing-optional (waitstaff are clothed). Club Orient received a direct hit from Hurricane Luis and today sports a fresh face. Sadly, though, much of the vegetation on this end of the beach was lost and it will be several years before it returns to its former state.

Esmeralda Resort, Orient Beach, ☎ 800-622-7836. $$-$$$. From the action-packed waters off Orient Beach, the green roofs of Esmeralda Resort are easy to spot. Fifteen villas, accommodating 65 guest rooms, are sprinkled across the low hills that rise gently from Baie Orientale. Each villa includes its own swimming pool; accommodations offer air-conditioning, satellite TV, telephones, fully equipped kitchenettes and private terraces. A poolside restaurant, L'Astrolabe, features continental cuisine.

Le Meridien's L'Habitation & Le Domaine, ☎ 800-543-4300. $$$. These two adjoining resorts are located on the island's northeast coast, tucked into Marcel Cove. Surrounded by a 150-acre nature preserve, they are landscaped with bougainvillea, hibiscus and oleander. Guest rooms, with bright Caribbean colors, include 251 rooms at L'Habitation with garden or marina views and 145 rooms and suites at the newer wing, Le Domaine. Facilities include swimming pools, private white sand beach and shuttle service to casinos, Philipsburg and Marigot. Watersports include deep-sea fishing, boating (motorboat, sail, power, catamaran and glass bottom), sailing, scuba diving, water skiing, canoeing, jet skiing, kayaking and more. Horseback riding, racquetball, squash, fitness center and tennis also available.

EARTH WATCH: *The Meridien hotels are no longer using chemicals on the plants to keep green fly, plant louse, etc. at bay. They now use ladybugs. They also have chickens roaming freely around the property to keep the centipedes away. The hotels are very conscious about conserving energy and water and actively advise their guests to do the same.*

Villas

Several villa rental companies offer travelers the option of staying in a fully furnished villa, complete with cooking facilities and plenty of room. Contact these companies for information (dial 011-590 first if calling from the US):

Carimo	☎ 87-57-58, fax 87-71-88
Immobilier St. Martin Caraibes	☎ 87-55-21
West Indies Immobilier	☎ 87-56-48
International Immobilier	☎ 87-79-00
Sprimtour	☎ 87-58-65
Interprom	☎ 87-32-46

St. Martin/Sint Maarten

Where to Eat

 French St. Martin offers all types of cuisine. Look for over 50 restaurants in Marigot, 20 in Grand Case and others in Cul de Sac, Mont Vernon and Orient Beach. French food reigns, but you'll also find Italian, Swiss and many other cuisines.

Reservations usually aren't necessary at lunch, but plan ahead for dinner, especially during busy winter months. Prices for a three-course meal without wine are high, as much as $50 or $60 per person at top restaurants. A good guide to local restaurants is *Ti Gourmet*, a free publication in French and English available from area hotels and the Tourist Office.

French

The Rainbow, Grand Case, ☎ 011-590-875580, $$$$. On the waterfront, this fine restaurant is one to save for your most special night out. With continental and French dishes, this eatery is the kind of place the two of you will talk about long after your vacation. Open nightly except Sundays.

Kontiki Orient Beach, Orient Beach, ☎ 011-590-874327, $$$. As its name suggests, this casual beach eatery takes a Polynesian approach, sort of a Gilligan's Island meets St. Tropez. You can't miss the big Easter Island-type statues at the beachside entrance. Inside, however, the menu is strictly French.

La Vie En Rose, Marigot, ☎ 011-590-87-54-42, $$$. Diners can enjoy an elegant meal in the upstairs restaurant of this French eatery or a traditional French experience at the sidewalk café.

Shopping

 The best shopping is in the capital city of **Marigot**. A crafts market near the cruise terminal offers jewelry, T-shirts, souvenir items, carvings and paintings (we were especially taken with the Haitian artwork available here). Marigot also is home to boutiques open 9 a.m. to 12:30 p.m. and 3 to 7 p.m., which offer liqueurs, cognacs, cigars, crystal, china, jewelry and perfumes, many from France. Up to $600 in goods may be brought back to the US by every member of your party without paying duty.

St. Martin/Sint Maarten

Dutch Sint Maarten

Out on the Island

Dutch Sint Maarten is distinctly more urbanized than its Gallic neighbor, the result of over 40 years in the tourism industry. Nonetheless, visitors find plenty of outdoor space to hike, bike, snorkel, scuba dive and, most especially, to boat.

Sint Maarten is located on the southern side of the island, an irregular shaped body of land that's punctuated by salt ponds and the immense **Simpson Bay**.

The eastern reaches of Sint Maarten overlook the Atlantic, from beaches such as Oyster Pond and Dawn Beach. These beaches are backed by roads that snake their way through a labyrinth of steep hills. Most notable is **Naked Boy Hill**, named after the legend of a former resident who lived on the hill and had no means of transportation other than walking. When he climbed, he took off his clothes so he wouldn't get them sweaty.

All the east side roads eventually lead to the capital city of **Philipsburg**, a narrow strip of a town tucked between Great Bay and the Great Salt Pond. The town is long and composed of just a few streets, primarily Frontstreet along the bayfront and Backstreet, one block over. The streets are connected by passages lined with shops.

Expect traffic to be slow going through Philipsburg just about any time of day. Narrow streets, plenty of cars and lots of pedestrians keep things at a crawl. Most visitors should plan to just walk from shop to shop, by far the easiest mode of transportation.

From Philipsburg the roads wind west toward Simpson Bay Lagoon and to the island's best lookout: **Cole Bay Hill**. A small snack bar (often with live music) is found at this scenic overlook which makes a great place for a morning photo of Simpson Bay Lagoon or a sunset lookout.

Downhill, the terrain flattens toward **Simpson Bay Lagoon**, the largest inland body of water in the Caribbean. Accessible by boats of all sizes beneath drawbridges on both the Dutch and French sides, this lagoon is home to vessels from around the globe. Sunset lagoon cruises are a popular option for viewing this body of water.

A narrow strip of land between Simpson Bay and Simpson Bay Lagoon is the site of **Princess Juliana International Airport**, the island's major airport. The road snakes its way around the airport to Maho Bay, on the western side of the island. This bay is right at the end of the runway (onlookers sometimes illegally hold onto the airport fence when the jumbo jets rev their engines. Gusts are strong enough to send onlookers airborne and last year blew an illegally parked car across the road.)

Maho Bay is the nightlife center of the island, home to the largest casino and several happening nightspots. Just north of Maho lies **Mullet Bay**, with an excellent snorkeling beach, the island's only golf course and a large resort still under renovation following damage from Hurricane Luis.

North of Mullet lies Cupecoy Beach, one of the island's most beautiful, right on the border between the French and the Dutch side.

Sint Maarten is currently undergoing an island beautification project, a package of 25 landscaping, construction and public works projects to enhance the island. "Our challenge is two-fold," said Theo Heyliger, St. Maarten's Commissioner of Tourism, Commerce and Economic Development. "We want to continue to improve overall physical conditions on the island for the benefit of both residents and visitors. At the same time we want to adopt a master plan and strict enforcement codes to sustain future growth and development."

The master plan includes long-term zoning regulations and stricter regulations on both public and private facilities. Some of the projects will include beautification and enhancement of Cyrus Wathey Square in downtown Philipsburg, landscaping sightseeing areas, preservation of historic Fort Amsterdam, establishment of a system of parks equipped with picnic and recreation areas, improvement of the island's roadway network, beautification of the Great Salt Pond in Philipsburg and adoption of strict maintenance regulations for island developers.

One of the largest projects is the $60 million port facility and entertainment complex and the downtown cruise pier. The new $2.5 million Captain Hodge Wharf in Philipsburg is a recent addition and the first phase in the plan.

Getting Around

Rental Cars & Taxi Service

Taxis are one of the best ways to get around the island, especially for the first-time visitor. The traffic in Philipsburg can be daunting so splurge and enjoy taxi transportation, at least for your first few days. Here's a sample of taxi rates around the island:

TAXI RATES

Princess Juliana Airport to Bobby's Marina	$10
Airport to Dawn Beach	$18
Airport to Maho Beach Resort	$5
Airport to Philipsburg	$8
Philipsburg to Marigot	$8

Taxis travel freely around the island, crossing back and forth over the border. You'll find taxis at the stand by the Courthouse in Philipsburg.

Taxi rates are set by the government. The minimum rate is $4 for one or two persons, with an extra $2 charged for each additional passenger. The cost rises after 10 p.m. (25% increase) and again after midnight (50% above daytime rates). Tips of 10 to 15% are customary.

Car Rental Companies

You'll find that most rental companies offer free pick up and delivery service. To rent a vehicle, you'll need a valid driver's license and a major credit card. Driving throughout the island is on the right side of the road.

Cost varies by type of car and operator, but expect to pay about $33 per day for a mid-size car. There are many car rental companies, as shown below (for all local numbers listed below, i.e., non-800 numbers, you must first dial 011-5995 if calling from the US).

St. Martin/Sint Maarten

Ambassador, Maho Beach Hotel   ☎ 52115, ext. 4406
Adventure, Princess Juliana Airport   ☎ 43688
Avis Car Rental, Colebay   ☎ 800-331-1084
Best Deal, Princess Juliana Airport   ☎ 53061
Budget Car and Trucks Rental   ☎ 800-527-0700
Cannegie, Airport & Frontstreet   ☎ 22397
Delta Car Rental, St. Jansteeg   ☎ 25733
Diamond, Princess Juliana Airport   ☎ 43003
Dollar Rent A Car, Bush Road   ☎ 24698
Donald's, Princess Juliana Airport   ☎ 54361
Economy Rent a Car, Genip Road   ☎ 22464
E&M Rent A Car, Bush Road   ☎ 22674
Empress Rent a Car, Atrium Resort   ☎ 71970
Explorer, Princess Juliana Airport   ☎ 42632
Fortuno Rent A Car, Cayhill   ☎ 23420
Hertz, Airport   ☎ 800-654-3001, ☎ 54314
Holiday Car Rental, Mullet Bay   ☎ 52801
J.C. Car Rental, Zaegersgmut Road   ☎ 22777
L.C. Fleming, Princess Juliana Airport   ☎ 54231
Lucky Car Rental, Colebay   ☎ 42268
Luti Rent A Car, Simpson Bay   ☎ 43538
National, Colebay Lagoon   ☎ 800-227-3876, ☎ 42168
Opel Car Rental, Point Blanch   ☎ 54324
Paradise Island, Princess Juliana Airport   ☎ 52361
Payless, Princess Juliana Airport   ☎ 52490
Regie's, Princess Juliana Airport Rd.   ☎ 52307
Risdon, Airport & Frontstreet   ☎ 23578
Roy Rogers, Airport & Simpson Bay   ☎ 52701
            ☎ 800-235-7727
Safari Rentals, Princess Juliana Airport Rd.   ☎ 53186
Sun & Fun, Princess Juliana Airport   ☎ 52706
Sunshine, Princess Juliana Airport Rd.   ☎ 52684
Trade Winds, Princess Juliana Airport Rd.   ☎ 53664

Public Buses

Public buses are available and are an inexpensive way to get around the island. The Dutch side is divided into three districts with varying fares. Buses run from about 5 a.m. to midnight.

At the Airport

The Princess Juliana International Airport is just east of Maho Bay on the southwest side of the island. A hub for many Caribbean flights, the modern airport is comfortable and has many conveniences including duty-free shopping.

Warning: When departing, do all your shopping **before** entering the departure area. Once you've passed into the departure area, you will not be allowed to return to the shops.

Beaches

There's plenty of action on St. Maarten's shores; the brochures like to say 37 beaches, one for each of the island's 37 square miles. **Mullet Bay Beach**, adjacent to the presently closed Mullet Bay Beach Resort, is perfect for swimming and snorkeling in gentle, protected waters. **Maho Beach**, at Maho Beach Resort and Casino, offers a totally different type of experience, with sometimes rough waters and a totally different kind of attraction: the dubious thrill of planes coming in for landing at what seem like yards from your head.

On the western side of the island, the most dramatic beach is **Cupecoy Beach**, near the border with the French side. This is the beach you'll often see in Sint Maarten brochures, featuring beautiful sea caves carved in the cliffs and offering silhouetted views of aquamarine waters against sunflower-toned sand. Many visitors come here to enjoy privacy and topless bathing (and, occasionally, nude bathing as well, although it is prohibited on the Dutch side.) To reach the beach, go down the concrete stairs (uneven, so watch out) near the parking area at Sapphire or continue down the dirt road past Sapphire, park at the end of the road and walk down. This route takes you closest to the sea caves for which Cupecoy is noted.

Little Bay Beach is a favorite with snorkelers. Calm waters mean good visibility except during a southeasterly wind. For a much quieter experience, try **Simpson Bay Beach,** where there are no resorts, no facilities and no crowds.

Dawn Beach, on the island's east side, is a favorite with wavehoppers and surf lovers. These waters can occasionally be too choppy

St. Martin/Sint Maarten

for swimming and too churned up for good snorkeling, but this beach has one of the island's best sunrise views. Nearby, Oyster Pond is where the legendary Frenchman and Dutchman started their walk around the island to divide the acreage between the two nations. Today the boundary makes an added attraction for beachlovers: you can swim between the French and Dutch sides in just a few strokes.

Dawn Beach.

Adventures

On Foot

Hiking

Mount Concordia, the site where French and Dutch representatives signed the agreement in 1648 to divide the island, is a symbol of relationship between these two nations. Every year a special ceremony remembers the anniversary of that treaty. For a good view, climb Mount Concordia, located in the center of the island.

Cole Bay Hill. Located west of Philipsburg, this scenic overlook is one of the best on the island and offers views of Anguilla, Saba, Sint Eustatius, St. Kitts and Nevis. A small bar is located at the overlook and down on the coast you can enjoy a walk from Cole Bay to Cay Bay, a trail that takes about an hour to walk.

On Wheels

Cycling

 Cyclists will find that Sint Maarten is challenging because of its rolling hills. For a relaxing ride, tour around Simpson Bay Lagoon. For a more rigorous workout, take the main road **around the island** (35 miles) for a view of the coastline. If you're into **mountain biking**, try your skills up **Paradise Peak** (on the French side), the island's highest point at 1,400 feet.

Bicycle Rentals

Bikes are available for rent from **Tri-Sports** on Airport Road at Simpson Bay. The cost is $15 per day or a weekly rate of $13 per day. Delivery and pick up are available. For information and reservations, ☎ 011-5995-54384.

On Water

Scuba Diving

 St. Maarten offers scuba diving for first-timers and advanced divers. Visibility ranges from 75 to 125 feet in these waters, which are home to a wide array of marine life. Waters are warm year-round, averaging 70°.

One popular site is the wreck of the British man-o-war *Proselyte* set on a reef a mile offshore. The 1801 wreck is located off Great Bay and still reveals its anchors and cannons. Another popular wreck dive is the *Teigland*, a freighter deliberately sunk in 1993 on Cable Reef. The site is home to many marine animals. Top reef diving is found nine miles offshore at a site called **Groupers**. Rates for single tank dives run about $45.

Dive Operators

Scuba operators include: **Dive St. Maarten**, Pelican Marina, ☎ 011-5995-42640; **Leeward Island Divers**, Welfare Rd., ☎ 011-5995-43320; **Ocean Explorers**, Simpson Bay, ☎ 011-5995-44357/44252; **Trade Winds Dive Center**, Great Bay Marina, ☎ 011-5995-75176.

Snorkeling

Good visibility makes snorkeling popular around St. Maarten's beaches. The top snorkel spot is **Little Bay Beach**, which has good reefs and calm waters (except when there's a southeast wind).

Snorkel trips are available from several operators. **Sand Dollar** (☎ 011-5995-42640 or contact your hotel activity desk) offers three-hour snorkel excursions to Creole Rock. Departing at 10 a.m. and 2 p.m. from Pelican Marina Tuesday through Saturdays, the trips include sightseeing through Simpson Bay Lagoon, Marigot Harbor, Friar's Bay, Happy Bay and Grand Case. Use of snorkel equipment, view boards and drinks are also included. The cost is $35 per person. Snorkel trips to Anguilla on a powerboat are also available for $70.

Watersports

You name it, you'll find it as far as watersports goes. Waverunners, catamarans, jet skis, parasailing, waterskiing, windsurfing, banana rides, beach toys, whatever. Watersports action is found primarily at **Cupecoy Beach** and **Simpson Bay**, a calm body of water popular with waterskiers. Boogie boarders head to **Guana Bay**, where shallows often have an undertow.

These operators offer various watersports activities:

Banana Hammock Watersports and Dive Center, Great Bay Beach Hotel and Casino (☎ 011-5995-22446, ext. 536): waverunners, catamarans, snorkeling, banana boat rides, waterskis.

Beach Mania, Cupecoy Beach (☎ 011-5995-52562): waverunners, jet skis, snorkeling, banana rides, beach rentals.

Land and Sea, Belair Beach Hotel (☎ 011-5995-23362, ext. 108): snorkeling and rafts for rent.

Pelican Watersports, Pelican Resort (☎ 011-5995-42640): boat rentals, waterskis, waverunners, sailing/snorkel trips, fishing.

Westport Watersports, Simpson Bay (☎ 011-5995-42557): banana boat, jet skis, parasailing, waterskiing, waverunners, windsurfing.

Fishing

Snapper, grouper, yellowtail, sailfish, kingfish, tuna, mahi mahi, wahoo, shark, barracuda and marlin are the goal of deep-sea charters available on a half- or full-day basis year-round. Good fishing is found not far offshore so anglers don't need to spend a lot of time traveling. Rates vary by operator and by the length of the trip. Look for prices averaging about $1,400 for a marlin trip, $1,000 for a full-day charter, $750 for a three-quarter-day charter and $575 for a half-day trip. Most operators include bait and equipment as well as beer, soft drinks and snacks.

Try your luck at a deep-sea catch with these operators: *Freedom*, Captain Oliver's Marina (☎ 011-5995-70031/42511); **Pelican Watersports**, Pelican Resort (☎ 011-5995-42640); **Rudy's**, Airport Road (☎ 011-5995-52177); **Fun in the Sun**, Great Bay Marina (☎ 011-5995-52481).

Yacht Charters

St. Maarten is a yachties' mecca. Both bareboat and crewed charters are available so that vacationers can take off either on a day trip or a longer voyage. Many yachts specialize in fine dining prepared by the crew using fresh ingredients picked up on daily tenders in neighboring islands. Crewed charters are available from these operators:

Bay Island Yachts	☎ 011-5995-42511; fax 42515
Bobby's Marina, Philipsburg	☎ 011-5995-22366
Captain Oliver's, Oyster Bay	☎ 011-5995-70031
Nicholson Yacht Charters	☎ 800-662-6066
Tradewinds Yachts	☎ 011-5995-42511
The Moorings	☎ 800-437-1880
Sunsail	☎ 800-327-2276
Pretty Woman	☎ 510-814-0400 or 011-5995-42511

We journeyed aboard a Bay Island yacht and can testify that it's the opportunity to live like a king. The company offers vessels from runabouts to 110-foot yachts for $5,500 per day with a crew of five. These large boats can accommodate 10 to 12 people and include a full assortment of water toys and a gourmet chef. Headquartered at the Simpson Bay Yacht Club, the 110-foot yacht includes a 33-foot tender, two jet skis, four staterooms and plenty of luxury.

St. Martin/Sint Maarten

On Your Own Boat

If you bring your own boat into Sint Maarten, you'll find first-class accommodations. For protection in storms, many sailors choose Simpson Bay Lagoon. Passage into the lagoon beneath raised drawbridges can be made from the windward French side or the Dutch leeward side. Moorings or slips are available at Simpson Bay Yacht Club, Island Water World, Great Bay Marina, Bobby's Marina and many others. Slip space runs between $6 and $7.50 per foot per month and most day rates range between 40¢ and 70¢ per foot. Most marinas offer water and electric hook-ups, dockside gasoline and around-the-clock dinghy service. Eight chandleries on the Dutch side offer maintenance and repairs.

Day Cruises

For many travelers, a good day's adventure is sailing around the island, a little snorkeling and a deck picnic or perhaps an elegant sunset sail to watch the lights come out in Dutch Sint Maarten.

Costs vary by activity and operator. Catamaran cruises run about $45 a person for a half-day sail and range from $50-$70 for a full-day cruise. Power boat excursions run about $95 for a full day. Sailboat cruises average about $65-$70 for a day sail. Lagoon cruises cost about $28 per person and dinner cruises run about $60.

Day Cruise Operators

Here's a list of boat and catamaran operators who offer regularly scheduled excursions:

Bluebeard Charters (☎ 011-5995-52898), Kim Sha Beach, full-day catamaran charters.

Panther Carib (book at your hotel activity desk), Great Bay Marina, 9:30-3:30 catamaran trips.

Golden Eagle (☎ 011-5995-30068), Great Bay Marina, four-hour catamaran excursions.

White Octopus motorized catamaran (☎ 011-5995-24096), Bobby's Marina in Philipsburg, full-day catamaran trips.

El Tigre (☎ 011-5995-42640), Pelican Resort, full-day catamaran trips.

Ulti-Mate (book at your hotel activity desk), Captain Oliver's Marina, full-day catamaran cruises.

Falcon (☎ 011-5995-22167), Great Bay Marina, full-day catamaran trips.

Swaliga (☎ 011-5995-22167), Great Bay Marina, full-day catamaran trips.

Lambada (☎ 011-5995-42640), Pelican Resort, all-day catamaran excursions.

Baja (book at your hotel activity desk), Stop and Shop on Airport Road, full-day powerboat trips.

Santino (☎ 011-5995-42503), Pelican Resort, full-day powerboat trips.

Sand Dollar (☎ 011-5995-42640), Pelican Resort, three-hour trips aboard a powerboat.

Lady Mary (☎ 011-5995-53792), Simpson Bay Lagoon, three-hour sunset dinner cruise.

The Explorer (☎ 011-5995-30068), dock on Airport Road, three hour cruising on the lagoon.

Sailing

If you'd like to learn to sail, Bay Island operates an American Sailing Association (ASA) sailing school . For information on sales or charters, racing and excursions, contact **Bay Island Yachts** at ☎ 011-5995-42511; fax 42515.

Serious sailors look at Sint Maarten as the home of one of the world's largest sailing events: the **Heineken Regatta**. Fun for spectators and competitors, this world-class event attracts hundreds of participants from Europe, the US and the Caribbean. Nearly 200 boats compete in nine classes: racing class, racing/cruising class (older boats or racer cruises), cruising class (non-spinnaker), fun class, bareboat class, multi-hull (open to all multi-hulls) and beach cat class.

Entries are taken by the St. Maarten Yacht Club. The fees are about $110 for all classes. The race spans three days. Day one begins in Philipsburg and ends in Marigot. Day two picks up in Marigot and returns to Philipsburg. Day three starts in Philipsburg and goes around the island to Simpson Bay.

But the race itself is just part of the fun. Pre-race activities include evening parties and an invitational 12-Meter Match off Great Bay where invited sailors race what are often termed the "greyhounds of the sea" in an exhibition event.

St. Martin/Sint Maarten

RACING FOR THE AMERICA'S CUP

"Primary grinders, stand by, first gear," the skipper shouted. We tightened our grip on the winch. "Primary grinders, go!" Suddenly, our arms were a blur as we, along with two other primary grinders, powered a winch to lift a massive Genoa sail into the wind. Our boat: the *Stars and Stripes*. Our mission: to win the America's Cup. Well, maybe not *the* America's Cup. This was the 12-Metre Challenge, a race for both first-time sailors and salty skippers alike, held three times daily, six days a week in the azure waters off Sint Maarten.

Thrilling action on the waves.

The Sint Maarten 12-Metre Challenge is the brainchild of Colin Percy, a Canadian businessman who moved to the Caribbean five years ago when "my doctor told me to slow down, that I needed a change of lifestyle." So, following a lifelong love of sailing that started at the age of seven, Percy moved to Sint Maarten. Locating in Philipsburg, he soon set about purchasing the most elite craft in the world of sailing: the 12-meter boats used in the America's Cup race. After buying the Canadian racers *Canada II* and *True North I* and *IV*, Percy set his sights on one of the best-known vessels in the world: Dennis Conner's *Stars and Stripes*, winner of the 1987 America's Cup. "Dennis Conner's decision for us to have the boat here gives American sailors a lot of pleasure. People who never thought they would set foot on an

America's Cup boat are emulating the America's Cup race," says Percy. When *Stars and Stripes '87* was moved to Sint Maarten, Conner estimated that only 30 sailors had ever raced aboard the vessel. Counting all the America's Cup boats, the numbers remain small. "Out of the millions of sailors around the world, there are no more than 700 very elite sailors who have raced America's Cup yachts," points out Percy. But we were not part of that group of seasoned sailors. Without even the experience of skippering a sunfish, we signed up for duty and soon found ourselves learning our task for the 45-minute race. Along with 16 fellow crewmates, we got our assignments from a crew that hailed from South Africa, Virginia and jolly old England.

With tanned skin and sunbleached hair, each crewmember looked the part of an America's Cup sailor and with good reason. "I wouldn't be at all surprised if we saw two or three of our sailors in the next America's Cup," says Percy. "There is no other venue in the world where young men and women in their late teens or early 20s can go sail these boats." Tested by Percy and chosen from applicants that number as many as 50 a day in peak season, the sailors know their jobs. And soon they taught us ours. We learned that this was no pleasure cruise – we were there to work. For the better part of an hour we practiced our jobs, tacking and jibing, kicking up a salty spray and often leaning so far into the wind that half the crew enjoyed a cool Caribbean bath. The division of labor was spread among the crew. A navigator kept us on the course (which ranges from eight to 12 miles, depending on wind conditions that day). A timekeeper ensured that we started the race without penalty. A hydraulics expert operated the hydraulic primer to control the boom and keep the sails tight. Backstay grinders and trimmers moved sails and ropes, as did mainsail grinders and trimmers. And the primary grinders? Using muscles long ignored, we powered the mighty genoa sail, setting it to catch the wind and power us ahead of our competitors. We had learned that the sail we controlled carried a price tag of $21,000. That was a real bargain compared with other parts on this Cadillac of boats: $67,000 for the rigging, $120,000 for the mast and $180,000 for a set of winches. But those financial

St. Martin/Sint Maarten

responsibilities paled in comparison to our real obligation: to win.

On that day, facing off against two Canadian rivals, we knew that Dennis was counting on us. "White flag up!" shouted our captain from the stern. In the actual America's Cup race, boats have 15 minutes to position themselves at the start, but, as Colin Percy had explained in our pre-race briefing, we could do it in less. So, with our crew that ranged from a 15-year-old boy from Massachusetts to a grandmother on a cruise shore excursion, we worked to maneuver *Stars and Stripes*. "White flag down!" We had only four minutes to the start. Pre-start maneuvers put us in position both to cross the start line on time and to block the wind from the other boats, effectively slowing them down. With the wind whipping as hard as 20 knots and swells churning up at six feet, we were quickly dowsed as we turned into position. "Blue flag up!" Three minutes. Another turn. Another cascade of Caribbean water into the boat. "Blue flag down!" One minute to race time. From over our shoulders, we could see *True North IV* and *Canada II* struggling into position, each trying to get upwind and closest to the starting line without crossing over. "Red flag up! Start!" The race was on.

We were now on course, racing upwind and zigzagging through the eye of the wind by tacking as fast as the crew could shout orders. Minutes later, we jibed around the windmark and began sailing downwind. *Canada II* had pulled into the lead, but we were just a boat-length behind. From our position we could see her masts, the height of an eight-story building, leaning into the wind. For 45 minutes, we edged both Canadian vessels for the lead. Finally, on the last stretch, *Stars and Stripes* pulled ahead. With one last "Primary grinders, go!" instruction, we were leading. And suddenly, there was one last shout. "Blue flag up!" Blue for *Stars and Stripes*. We had won. Dennis would be proud.

The 12-Metre Challenge is at Bobby's Marina in Philipsburg. Wear soft-soled running shoes and a t-shirt and shorts over a swimsuit. Bring along sunscreen. You will get wet. There is a storage area in the hull for backpacks and bags. There is no restroom on board. Complimentary cold drinks (water, soft drinks and beer) are available on board. The regatta takes two hours, including the race. The cost of the regatta is $60 US per person. For information or reservations, write the **Sint Maarten 12-Metre Challenge**, PO Box 2064, St. Maarten, Netherlands Antilles, Caribbean, ☎ 011-5995-43354.

Ferry Service

Sint Maarten's proximity to other members of the Leeward Islands give vacationers the opportunity to visit St. Barts and Saba (take a day trip to Anguilla from Marigot in French St. Martin). **The Edge Ferry Service** offers two excursions. Travel to Saba, the tiny island that's really a volcanic peak, on Wednesday, Friday and Sunday. Departure is at 9 a.m. from Pelican Marina at Simpson Bay; return is at 5 p.m. The trip takes one hour and costs $60 round-trip. For a Gallic experience, travel to nearby St. Barts (or St. Barths), a 45-minute excursion aboard the ferry. The 9 to 5 trip runs Tuesday, Thursday and Saturday; cost is $50 round-trip plus a $7 port charge. For information or reservations on either trip, ☎ 011-5995-42640/42503, ext. 1553; fax 011-5995-42476.

In the Air

Sky Diving

Well, this is one adventure that you just don't find on every island. **Tandem Skydiving** (☎ 011-5995-75634 or 52206) offers visitors the opportunity to jump out of a perfectly good airplane for no reason other than the thrill of it. After a short briefing, riders are strapped to an experienced skydiver, then it's bon voyage from 9,000 feet. The ride whizzes by at 120 miles per hour and takes about 30 seconds.

Parasailing

If you'd like to have a bird's-eye view of Simpson Bay, visit **Westport Watersports** (☎ 011-5995-42557) at Kim Sha Beach on Simpson Bay.

On Horseback

 Two operators offer horseback rides and lessons. **Horse-N-Around** (☎ 011-5995-42465) has horses, miniature horses and ponies. Open Monday through Saturday, 8-5; closed Sundays. **Crazy Acres** (☎ 011-5995-42793) has horses and ponies. Open Monday through Saturday, 9-2; closed Sundays.

Other Sports

Golf

 Mullet Bay, the hotel closed by Hurricane Luis and at press time still closed, is home to an 18-hole golf course that's back in operation. The championship course, designed by Joseph Lee, includes a putting green and practice green. Greens fees include a golf cart and run about $105 for 18 holes or $60 for nine holes; club rentals available for $20-$25. Reservations should be made about a week in advance; ☎ 011-5995-52801 or 5995-53069.

Jogging

The **Road Runners Club of St. Maarten** has a Fun Run every Wednesday at 5 p.m. and invites visitors. On Sundays, an early bird run of two to 15K starts at 6:45 a.m. at the Pelican Resort and Casino. Contact the front desk at Pelican Resort (☎ 011-5995-42503) for more information.

Sightseeing

The capital city of **Philipsburg** bustles with activity in its duty-free shops and glitzy casinos, but still boasts plenty of history. The town's Frontstreet has been a market since the 17th century, when Dutch traders brought their acquisitions to the island from as far away as Indonesia.

Courthouse. The most distinctive structure in town, this green and white building was built in 1793 and renovated just a few years ago. It's a popular meeting site for shoppers on Frontstreet and the taxi stand is nearby.

St. Maarten Museum, 119 Frontstreet, Philipsburg. Housed in a restored 19th-century West Indian house in downtown Philipsburg, this museum features the history and culture of the island. Displays include artifacts from prehistoric to modern times. Open 9 to 4 weekdays and 9 to noon on Saturdays. Admission, $1.

Where to Stay

Hotels & Resorts

 Holland House Beach Hotel, Philipsburg, ☎ 800-223-9815, 011-5995-22572. $. This 54-room hotel is the ideal location for serious shoppers. Especially popular with Dutch travelers in town to do business in Philipsburg, this charming European-style hotel is also perfect for those looking to do a little business of their own in the duty-free shops. The junior suite here is an excellent value, two rooms with kitchen, living room and a large balcony.

Maho Beach Hotel and Casino, Simpson Bay, ☎ 800-223-0757. $$. This 600-room hotel is within walking distance of plenty of action if you are looking for nightlife. A high-rise built around a sprawling freshwater pool, this resort is at the heart of the night scene because it is home to the island's largest casino and just across the street from one of its most popular nightspots: Cheri's Café. However, we found many members of the resort staff less than personable and encountered difficulties several times during our stay.

Divi Little Bay, ☎ 800-367-3484. $$. Perched on a peninsula between Great Bay and Little Bay, this newly reopened property offers spectacular views. The 159-room resort offers typical hotel rooms as well as studios and one-bedroom units. Facilities include a restaurant, pool and water activities center.

Great Bay Beach Hotel, Philipsburg, ☎ 800-613-1511. $$$. Ten minutes from downtown Philipsburg, this 285-room hotel offers visitors 24-hour fun. Daytime activities include watersports (wave runners, sailboats, windsurfing, snorkeling, paddleboats), tennis, beach and two swimming pools. In the evening hours, the Chrysalis Night Club is open every evening and the Golden Casino opens nightly at 8 p.m. Rates are all-inclusive, with transfers, three meals daily, drinks by the glass, sunset cruise, sightseeing tour, windsurfing, snorkeling, sailing, scuba clinic and more.

Small Inns

Passanggrahan, Philipsburg, ☎ 011-5995-23588. $-$$. Right on Philipsburg's Frontstreet, this traditional inn lavishes guests with a relaxed colonial atmosphere that rings true: this was once the governor's residence. Today it offers 26 guest rooms and four suites with Indonesian art and antiques.

Mary's Boon, Simpson Bay, ☎ 800-696-8177, 713-781-3399, 011-5995-54235. $$. This historic hideaway is near the airport. Facing Turquoise Bay, all 15 beachfront studios include verandahs, in-room cable TV, air-conditioning, ceiling fans, kitchenettes and more.

White Sands Beach Club, Simpson Bay, ☎ 800-616-1190. $. This quaint hideaway on Simpson Bay is for those looking to get away from it all: including the phones. Eleven beachfront units, ranging in size from beachfront chalets to two-bedroom cottages, are for couples only.

Condos & Villas

Beachside Villas, Simpson Bay, ☎ 011-5995-54294. $$$. These 13 luxury villas are on the beach at Simpson Bay.

Cupecoy Beach Club, ☎ 800-622-7836. $$. This condo/villa resort is perched on a cliffside overlooking a beach at Cupecoy. The 60 guest units include one-, two- and three-bedroom suites with fully equipped kitchens. A beach bar is on site.

Point Pirouette Villas, Mullet Bay, ☎ 800-223-9815. $$$+. These waterfront villas are on a privately owned peninsula near Mullet Bay. The 15 units include kitchenettes, washer and dryer. Guest facilities include a swimming pool and tennis courts.

VILLA RENTAL COMPANIES

Caribbean Concepts	☎ 800-423-4433
Caribbean Resorts and Villas	☎ 800-955-8180
Condo and Villa Authority	☎ 800-831-5512
Coral Shore Villas	☎ 800-942-6725
Island Properties	☎ 800-738-9444
Leslie's Vacation Villas	☎ 800-888-0897
Unusual Villas and Island Rental	☎ 804-288-2823
Vacation Home Rentals	☎ 800-633-3284

Where to Eat

 Dutch Sint Maarten doesn't often receive the rave restaurant reviews awarded to French St. Martin, but that's a mistake. With culinary offerings that range from French to Indonesian to Italian, this part of the island offers excellent dining at prices that are often better than the French section. Restaurants throughout the island reflect the many cultures that live here and the many lands which the Netherlands once influenced.

KESHI YENA

One of the Dutch Antilles' most distinct dishes is Keshi Yena, an Edam cheese stuffed with chicken.

Ingredients: *1 4-lb Edam cheese; 2 tablespoons butter or margarine; 2 lbs chicken, cooked, deboned and chopped; 2 medium onions, chopped; 1 large green bell pepper, chopped; 3 large tomatoes, chopped; 1 tablespoon chopped parsley; ½ teaspoon salt; 1 or 2 hot peppers, minced; cup unseasoned dry breadcrumbs; ¼ cup raisins; 2 tablespoons pickle relish; ½ cup chopped pimento-stuffed Spanish olives; 2 eggs, beaten.*

Peel the wax away from the cheese. Cut top off cheese casing and set it aside. Scoop out the cheese and reserve, leaving only the ½-inch shell. Cover the shell and top with water; soak for one hour and then drain.

Melt the butter in a medium saucepan. Add chicken, onion, bell pepper, tomatoes, parsley, salt and hot pepper. Sauté about five minutes. In a bowl, shred the reserved Edam and mix half with the breadcrumbs, raisins, pickle relish, olives and eggs, reserving the remaining cheese for another use.

Thoroughly combine the chicken mixture with the egg mixture. Preheat the oven to 350° F. Grease a three-quart casserole pan. Press the stuffing into the cheese shell and replace the top. Set stuffed shell in the casserole dish and bake 45 minutes.

Let the stuffed cheese stand for 10 minutes, then peel away and discard the outer skin. Cut in wedges and serve hot. Makes six to eight servings.

American

Cheri's Café, Maho Bay. $-$$. This lively nightspot is also open for lunch and dinner (until midnight) and features American favorites such as burgers and sandwiches as well as pasta specials, seafood, grilled steaks and chicken.

Argentinean

Rancho Argentinean Grill, ☎ 011-5995-52495. $$-$$$. Housed in a thatched-roof building, this large restaurant serves up Argentinean delights. Start with sangria or wine and some *empanadas* or *chorizos criollos* (Argentinean grilled sausage), then continue with the house specialty: steak. Sirloin, tenderloin, rib eye and T-bone are served with side orders such as *cebollas fritas* (fried onions), *maiz choclo* (grilled corn on the cob), *arroz criollo* (seasoned rice) or *plantos fritos* (fried plantains).

Caribbean

Lynette's, Simpson Bay, (011) 5995-52865, $$. The King Beau Beau Show, a calypso revue, livens this restaurant every Tuesday and Friday night. Any evening, however, you can find island favorites on the menu: Creole dishes, lobster, steak, fish and more.

Continental

Saratoga, Simpson Bay Yacht Club, ☎ 011-5995-42421, $$$. Right at the yacht club, this elegant restaurant has an ever-changing menu that highlights local ingredients: wild mushroom bisque of fish soup, grilled mahi-mahi with mustard sauce, sautéed red snapper fillet with garlic-white wine sauce or grilled duck breast, basmati rice and roasted yellow pepper sauce.

Dutch

Holland House, Philipsburg, ☎ 011-5995-22572. $$. Dine on veal wiener schnitzel, beef brochette, duck à l'orange or Dutch pea soup at this waterfront restaurant in the Holland House Beach Hotel. We especially enjoyed the appetizers.

French

Le Bec Fin, Frontstreet, Philipsburg, ☎ 011-5995-25725/22976. $$. This seaside restaurant has a casual downstairs eatery for breakfast and lunch and an upstairs section for an elegant dinner. Grilled lobster flambée, marinated duck breast, soufflés and more tempt evening visitors. The lunch crowd enjoys quiche, burgers, fish sandwiches and Neptune salads with sea scallops.

L'Escargot, 84 Frontstreet, Philipsburg, ☎ 011-5995-22483. $$-$$$. Located right on busy Frontstreet, this French eatery features, you guessed it, escargot. Try the snails in garlic butter, in cherry tomatoes, baked in mushroom caps or cooked up in an omelet. Seafood includes yellowtail filet sautéed in lemon butter, snapper in red wine sauce or shallots and lobster. The specialty dish is *canard de l'escargot*, a crisp duck in pineapple and banana sauce and winner of an award from *Gourmet* magazine. Open Monday through Friday for lunch and dinner; dinner only on weekends.

Indonesian

Wajang Doll, Philipsburg, ☎ 011-5995-22687. $$. *Rijstaffel* is the order of the day at this delightful eatery that serves up delicious Indonesian dishes to satisfy even the pickiest of eaters. Choose from a 14- or 19-dish spread. *Rijsttafel* or "rice table," an Indonesian feast, creates an evening of entertainment. Come with a big appetite. The meal begins with an appetizer of egg rolls followed by main courses such as *sateh ajam*, skewered chicken covered with a spicy peanut-flavored sauce, *kerrie djawa* (beef curry), *daging ketjap* (beef braised in soy and ginger sauce) and *telor* (egg in spiced coconut sauce.)

Seafood

Chesterfields Restaurant, Philipsburg, ☎ 011-5995-23484. $-$$. Enjoy a yacht club atmosphere in this casual eatery which offers many excellent seafood dishes. Both indoor and outdoor seating is available.

Thai

Passanggrahan, Philipsburg, ☎ 011-5995-23588, $$. This guest house serves up a spicy menu: jumbo prawns Marco Polo (red and green bell peppers in cream sauce flamed with Pernod), Pla Pow (grilled whole snapper with Thai seasoning) and Thai chicken curry.

Shopping

 In **Philipsburg**, shops line **Frontstreet**, the narrow boulevard nearest the waterfront. In these duty-free stores, electronic goods, leather, jewelry and liquor (especially guavaberry liqueur) are especially good buys. (For the best prices, shop on days when the cruise ships are not in port.) No duties are charged in or out of port (one of the few such ports in the world), so savings on consummer goods run about 25-50% at this popular duty-free stop. Shop carefully, though, and know prices on specific goods before you leave home. Some items are not bargains. Typically, shops open at 8 or 9 a.m. and remain open until noon, then reopen from 2 to 6 daily. When cruise ships are in port, most shops remain open through the lunch hours.

Philipsburg's Frontstreet invites browsing.

Nightlife

There's no denying that the Dutch side of the island is the nightlife capital. Fun occurs around the clock on this side of the island in both casinos and pulsating nightclubs.

Nine casinos are found on the Dutch side (there are no casinos on the French side). The largest is **Casino Royale** at the Maho Beach Hotel and Casino. Over two dozen individual tables operate from 1 p.m. to 4 a.m. every day of the year. The atmosphere is elegant and fun, starting with the cigar bar at the entrance and continuing to high stakes blackjack and craps tables inside.

The **Atlantis Casino** at Cupecoy Beach offers a private gaming room for high stakes players, with baccarat, French roulette, chemin de fer and seven-card stud poker.

There are four casinos in Philipsburg along busy Frontstreet. **Coliseum Casino, Diamond Casino, Neptune Casino** and **Rouge and Noire Casino** offer everything from video poker to Caribbean stud poker.

Sports lovers flock to **Lightning Casino** on Airport Road to place bets on boxing, baseball, soccer, hockey, football, basketball and horse racing shown on giant closed circuit TVs. **Pelican Casino** at the Pelican Resort in Simpson Bay offers slots, roulette, craps and blackjack and **Golden Casino** at Great Bay Beach Hotel features gaming tables and slots.

Cheri's Café, near Maho Bay Hotel, is one of the island's hottest night spots, with live music nightly. The open-air restaurant and bar pulsates with live music and is a favorite with locals and visitors.

Another happening spot is the **News Music Café**. The doors open at 9:30, but the action doesn't gear up until near midnight. This spot is a favorite for the latest music hits.

St. Barts

What's Special About It?

Whether you call it St. Barts, St. Barth or St. Barthélemy, you'll find this charming island to be très chic. At just eight square miles, this isle packs a lot of punch in the world of the glitterati, perhaps more than any other Caribbean destination. Especially during the peak winter months, don't be surprised to see celebrities wandering the streets of Gustavia, enjoying a glass of fine French wine in an open-air restaurant or puttering around the island in a little vehicle called a Mini-Moke.

English anchor at Bicentenary Square.

Without a doubt, St. Barts attracts the high-end market and its prices reflect this. Prices are some of the highest in the Caribbean. A look at the merchandise of the little shops in the capital city of Gustavia will confirm this.

But St. Barts does have a somewhat different package to offer. Much more so than French St. Martin, this island is rich with the spirit of French élan. While you'll find that shopkeepers, taxi drivers and restaurateurs speak English and the American dollar is welcomed most places, this is definitely an outpost of France. Enjoy a taste of Europe with a hearty dash of Caribbean sunshine.

St. Bart visitors fall into two categories: day trippers and overnighters. Day trippers arrive, by prop plane or by boat, from St. Martin to enjoy a morning and afternoon of shopping, touring and lunch at one of the many French eateries. Overnighters are typically well-heeled, eager for the exclusive getaway that this island can provide.

History

Discovered by Christopher Columbus in 1493 and named for his brother Bartolomeo, this small island was first settled around 1648 by French colonists who were living on St. Kitts. Things didn't work out with that early settlement and in 1651 the island was sold to the Knights of Malta. Five years later it was raided by the fierce Carib Indians and then was abandoned until 1673, when French from Normandy and Brittany tried settlement again.

Success met the settlers this time around. The island did well financially, aided by the bounty of many French buccaneers. Monbars the Exterminator, a famous buccaneer, reputedly maintained headquarters in St. Barts and his treasure is believed to be hidden among the coves of Anse du Gouverneur or buried in the sands of Grande Saline.

Unlike other Caribbean islands, St. Barts did not have a plantation economy. There were some small farms on the island during this time, but it did not have the plantations of its neighbors. Because of this, it did not have the slave population found on other islands and to this day few people trace their ancestry back to the African slaves.

In 1758 the island was taken over briefly by the British, but otherwise remained French. In 1784 one of Louis XVI's ministers sold the isle to Sweden in exchange for trading rights in Gothenburg. The Swedes moved onto the island renamed the harbor Gustavia. France finally repurchased the island in 1878.

TIMELINE

1493 European discovery by Christopher Columbus.

1648 First French colony.

1651 Island sold to the Knights of Malta.

1656 Carib Indians raid island.

1673 Settlers from Normandy and Brittany arrived.

1758 British briefly take over island.

1784 France sells island to Sweden.

1878 France repurchases island.

Geography & Land

Situated just below the Tropic of Cancer, St. Barts occupies just eight square miles in the Caribbean Sea. The island is hilly and rugged, topped by wooded areas with low-growing foliage. Cacti as well as tropical flowers punctuate the hillsides, which fall to meet the sea with 22 beaches that range in tone from white to pink to gold.

Climate

St. Barts' temperatures vary from 72 to 86° F. The island boasts 300 days of sunshine a year.

Flora & Fauna

Iguanas are commonly seen around the island, sunning themselves on a rock or in the road. The unofficial mascot of the island, however, is the **pelican**, often seen diving for its lunch in the surrounding waters. Seen more and more often is the **sea turtle**, which is protected by marine law.

St. Barts' flora and fauna is diverse. Look for bougainvillea, purple allamanda, golden trumpet, hibiscus, oleander and other tropical plants. This is not a lush island like St. Kitts and Nevis, but more

St. Barts

similar in topography and rainfall to St. Martin. Cacti and succulents are seen often on the hilly terrain.

In the sea, divers have a chance to enjoy St. Barts' rich marine life. Nurse sharks, rays, lobster, yellowtail snapper, spotted eagle rays, dorado and more are found off St. Barts' shores.

Government & Economy

St. Barts is a dependency of the island of Guadeloupe, which is an Overseas Department and Region of France. Residents participate in French elections just as if they resided in mainland France.

The island has a mayor who is elected every seven years, a town constable and a security force consisting of six policemen and 13 gendarmes sent from France on two-year tours of duty. St. Barts and French St. Martin are a Sous-Préfecture of Guadeloupe, which is administered by a Sous-Préfect, who resides in St. Martin and has a representative on St. Barts.

People & Culture

St. Barts is truly unique in the Caribbean. This island is the only one in the region with Swedish heritage. Today, most French-speaking islanders are descendants of the Norman, Breton and Poitevin settlers. It's a heritage that's still very much part of the present. On some parts of the island a few remaining older women wear enormous sunbonnets called *quichonette* ("kiss me not") and spend their days weaving straw hats and baskets.

This island also has many ties with the island of St. Thomas. In the mid-1950s, many St. Barts residents relocated to that US Virgin Island because of its burgeoning tourism industry. Even today a large French colony is near Charlotte Amalie, the largest colony of St. Barts natives living off island.

Approximately 6,000 people reside on St. Barts.

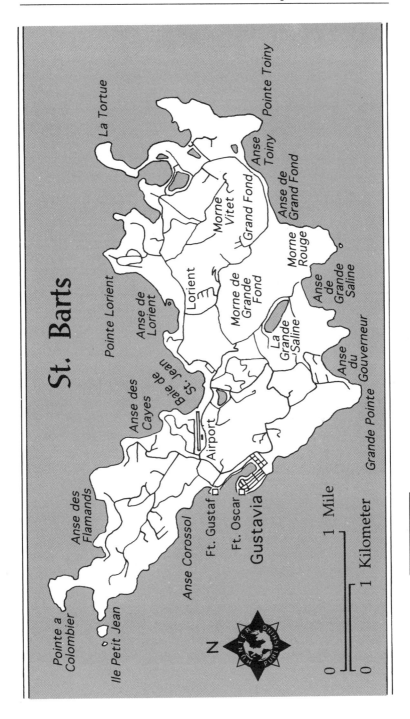

St. Barts

Travel Information

When to Go

Weather varies little throughout the year, just a few degrees from winter to summer. The biggest factor in deciding when to visit St. Barts is your pocketbook. Prices vary 40 to 50% from winter to summer. Low prices extend from mid-April through mid-December.

Customs

Customs are no problem in St. Barts; vacationers can enter with items appropriate for their stay. Day trippers on boats from St. Martin do not pass through Customs and Immigration on either end of their journey.

Cost

St. Barts is one of the most expensive islands in the Caribbean. Meal and accommodation prices are higher than those found on most other islands. Look for accommodations prices to average from $300-$700 during peak season. Lunch can easily run $50 per person and dinner even more. Budget travelers will find some less expensive options, however, especially by traveling in off-peak months.

Holidays

If you happen to be on-island for one of these festivals, be sure to take time and enjoy it!

CALENDAR OF EVENTS

◆ *January*
Jan. 1. **New Year's Day.**
Jan. 5. **Three Kings Day.** "Galette des rois," celebrated with Epiphany cake.
St. Barts Music Festival. Two weeks of music ranging from jazz to chamber music to opera, with concerts in Gustavia and Lorient.

◆ *February*
Carnival. Mardi Gras costumed parades and partying in Gustavia; Ash Wednesday burning of Vaval (King Carnival) at Shell Beach. Most businesses closed.

◆ *March*
Arts and Artisant. Show of St. Barts arts and crafts in Gustavia.
Mi-Carême or **Mid-Lent.** A day-long respite from fasting during Lenten period.
Easter.

◆ *April*
Festival Gastronomique of St. Barts. Presentations of regional wine and cooking from France at select island hotels and restaurants.
St. Barts Film Fête and **Caribbean Cinémathèque.** A five-day salute to Caribbean films and filmmakers.

◆ *May*
May 1. **Labor Day.** Public holiday.
May 8. **Armistice Day.** Public holiday.
Ascension Thursday. Public holiday.
Pentecost Monday. Public holiday.
May 27. **Slavery Abolition Day.** Public holiday.

◆ *June*
Underwater Film Festival.

St. Barts

◆ *July*

July 14. **Bastille Day**. French national holiday.

Festival of the North Villages. Beach part at Flamands with regattas, sports competitions, music, fireworks.

◆ *August*

Aug. 15. **Assumption Day**, St. Barts/Pitea Day. Commemorates the 1977 twinning of St. Barts and Pitea, Sweden. Sailing Regatta. Public holiday.

Festival of Gustavia. Dragnet fishing contest, dances, parties.

Festival of St. Barthélemy. Patron saint feast day. Regatta, dining, fireworks, public ball.

Feast of St. Louis. In village of Corossol with fishing festival, windsurfing contest.

Fête du Vent. Dragnet fishing contest, dances, parties in village of Lorient.

◆ *November*

Nov. 1. **All Saints Day**. Cemeteries decorated with hundreds of lighted candles. Public holiday.

Nov. 11. **Armistice Day** (WWI). Public holiday.

Swedish Marathon Race. Annual 2, 10, 15 km. races for all.

◆ *December*

Dec. 25. **Christmas**

Dec. 31. **Réveillon de la Saint Sylvestre**. New Year's Eve galas.

Transportation

By Plane

Most arrivals in St. Barts come through Sint Maarten, with connection to an inter-island flight or boat. It's a 10-minute hop from Sint Maarten's Princess Juliana International Airport on **Windward Islands Airways** (☎ 800-634-4907) or **Air St.**

Barthélemy (☎ 011-590-27-71-90), which also has flights from San Juan, Guadeloupe and Espérance Airport on French St. Martin. **Air Guadeloupe** (☎ 011-590-27-61-90) flies from Espérance on French St. Martin as well as Guadeloupe (one hour flying time) and St. Thomas (a 45-minute flight offered several times a week). **Air St. Thomas** (☎ 011-590-27-71-76) flies to St. Barts from San Juan via St. Thomas. Charter flights are available with Air St. Barthélemy, Windward Island Airways and **Air Caraibes** (☎ 011-590-27-99-41).

By Boat

Visitors can also explore St. Barts as a day trip from St. Martin. Take a quick trip aboard the *Voyager 2*, which departs from Marigot to Gustavia, St. Barts at 9 a.m. and 5:45 p.m. daily (reservations required for Sunday departure). The 1½-hour trip aboard the high-speed boat is comfortable, air-conditioned and includes a stocked bar. Round-trip is $50 plus a $9 tax. A package including lunch and an island tour is available for $80 plus a $9 tax. Considering the dining prices on St. Barts, it's a real bargain. Car rental is available for day trippers as well for $40. For reservations or information, call Corine or Philip at ☎ 011-590-87-20-28; fax 011-590-87-20-78.

From Grand Case on French St. Martin, St. Barth Commuter offers day trips to nearby St. Barthélemy. Flights depart on Wednesdays from Grand Case at 9 a.m. and return at 4:30 p.m. Round-trip air fare, including taxes, is US $80. A minimum of six participants, maximum of nine, is required. Bookings are accepted only until the preceding Monday at 3 p.m. For information, contact **St. Barth Commuter**, Customer Service, Aeroport de Grand Case, ☎ and fax 011-590-87-75-70.

St. Barts

Entry Requirements

Citizens of the US and Canada need either a passport or other proof of citizenship, such as a notarized birth certificate or a voter's registration card accompanied by some form of photo identification (a driver's license will do).

A departure tax of 30 FF ($5) is charged to all passengers.

Special Concerns

Currency

The French franc (FF) is legal tender, but US dollars are widely accepted. The exchange rate is roughly 6 FF to the 1 US dollar.

Language

French is the official language of St. Barts and locals speak a type of French that's an old Norman dialect. Most people, including shopkeepers and restaurant staff, speak English.

Dress

St. Barts is very casual: shorts, T-shirts and sandals. But don't expect just any shorts and T-shirts; this is a chic destination, with designer names to match. Evenings are dress-up time when well-heeled guests pull out all the stops (men do not need jackets and ties, however).

Electricity

Voltage is 220 AC, 60 cycles. American-made appliances require a transformer as well as French plug converters.

Telephones

To dial a St. Barts number from the US, first dial 011, then area code (590), then the number. To dial the US from St. Barts, dial 00, wait for another tone, then dial 1, area code and number. Note that phone prices are *expensive*: a one-minute call to the US runs 12.85 FF (almost $3).

Health

There's no need to take any special precautions for St. Barts; tap water is safe to drink, although bottled water is often served in restaurants. Gustavia has a clinic. There is no recompression chamber on the island.

Restrooms

You'll find public restrooms near the Gustavia harbor next door to the visitors center. The restrooms are unisex and include showers.

Tipping

Tips of 10-15% are traditional. Some restaurants and hotels add a 10% gratuity, so check before paying. Porters and bellhops usually receive 50¢ per bag. Taxi drivers receive 10-15% of the fare.

Marriage

Marriage is no simple feat on St. Barts. Foreigners need to show birth certificates (with raised seal), certificate of good conduct (including certification of single status), residency card (one of the two must have resided on the island for at least one month) and a medical certificate that includes a blood test issued within the last three months. All documents must be translated into French. A Bulletin de Mariage and Livret de Famille are delivered at the ceremony. There is no fee.

Sources of Information

Before your trip, contact **France on Call**, a toll service (50¢ per minute) operated by the French government (☎ 1-900-990-0040) for brochures and information or write the French Government Tourist Office nearest you:

444 Madison Ave.
New York, NY 10022

9454 Wilshire Blvd., Suite 715
Beverly Hills, CA 90212
☎ (310) 271-6665

676 N. Michigan Ave., Suite 3360
Chicago, IL 60611
☎ (312) 751-7800

1981 Ave. McGill College (490)
Montreal, Quebec H3A 2W9
☎ (514) 288-4264

30 St. Patrick St., Suite 700
Toronto, Ontario M5T 3A3
☎ (416) 593-6427

St. Barts

While on the island, stop by the visitors center in Gustavia. The Office du Tourisme is on the Quai Général de Gaulle, just steps from the harbor. The office is open 8:30 a.m. to 6 p.m., Monday through Friday, and 8:30 to noon on Saturdays during peak season; somewhat shorter hours during summer months. Stop by for brochures and maps in both French and English and helpful assistance about any tourist needs.

While on island, you can pick up a good deal of free information about what's happening. Both *Le Journal de St. Barth* and *St. Barth Magazine*, available at the tourism office, include good information. *Ti Gourmet* offers tips on dining.

Another good source of information is the Saint Barthélemy Web site: http://www.st-barths.com.

Out on the Island

Whether you call it St. Barts, St. Barth or Saint Barthélemy, the island is the same: small, très chic and secluded. Accessible only by a 20-seater plane or by boat, this French outpost is a getaway for the rich and famous.

St. Barts is shaped somewhat like a boomerang, with the two ends facing northward. The capital city of **Gustavia** is on the southwestern side of the island and boasts one of the prettiest harbors in the Caribbean. The U-shaped harbor is dotted with yachts whose white sails pose a stark contrast to the green hills punctuated by traditional red roofs around the town.

Northwest of Gustavia lies the community of **Colombier**, home of many older women who still can be seen wearing traditional clothing, such as the white bonnet. On the beach is the village of **Corossol**, home to many of the island's fishermen.

North of Gustavia, you can travel across the island to the community of **Saint Jean**, site of the island's first hotel. Today this region is where you will find many of the island's watersports on the **Baie de St. Jean**. East of St. Jean lies the community of Lorient, a small village on the beautiful Anse de Lorient. Continuing east, **Marigot** is where many of the island's gourmet restaurants are found. This region is also the location of some of the island's most beautiful bays and beaches: Anse de Marigot, Grand Cul de Sac and Petit Cul de Sac.

South of here lies **Grand Fond**, a favorite stop for scuba divers. With just 200 residents, this village has many traditional limestone homes.

Getting Around

Car Rentals & Taxi Service

If this is your first visit to St. Barts, spend a day or two splurging on taxi service. St. Barts is a steep, hilly island criss-crossed with winding, narrow roads. Until you have the lay of the land, let someone else do the driving. Rental cars and gasoline are both expensive options.

A flat taxi rate of 25FF (about $5) is set for taxi runs up to five minutes long. For each additional three minutes, the fare is increased by 20FF (about $4). Night fares are higher, as are fares on Sundays and holidays.

Two taxi stands are found on the island. One is at the airport and the other is in Gustavia on rue de la République. To call a taxi for pick up, dial 27-66-31 on island.

Car Rental Companies

St. Barts' airport has only a short landing strip so nothing larger than a 20-seater can land (and, even then, only in the daytime). The terminal offers a few amenities, including a car rental booth and a few shops.

Car reservations should be made in advance, especially in peak winter months. Most cars are VW Beetles or small Mini-Mokes – a combination beach buggy and convertible. All cars are stick shift. The speed limit is 28 mph (45 km/h).

Driving is not easy here because of hilly roads, sharp turns and narrow roads. Gustavia, although small, has an amazing amount of traffic and in mid-day is often bumper to bumper.

Rental cars average about $60 a day in the winter months, falling to about $35 a day during the summer. Major credit cards are

St. Barts

accepted but most agencies request a two- or three-day minimum rental. Rates include unlimited mileage, collision damage insurance (first $500 deductible) and free delivery.

Gas is another part of the rental car expense: look for prices about $3.25 per gallon. There are only two gas stations; both are closed on Sundays. An automatic gas pump has opened at the airport station. It can use magnetically sensitized cards that sell for 50FF (about $9).

Car rentals are available from these operators (dial 011 from US before number):

Mathieu Aubin, Vitet   ☎ 590-27-73-03 or 590-27-71-98
Avis, Airport   ☎ 590-27-71-43
Odette Brin, Terre Neuve   ☎ 590-27-63-99
Budget, Airport and Gustavia   ☎ 590-27-67-43
Europcar, Colombier,   ☎ 590-27-73-33
Charles Gréaux, Gustavia   ☎ 590-27-61-90
Edmond Gumbs, Colombier   ☎ 590-27-75-32
Hertz, Airport   ☎ 590-27-71-14
Ernest Lédée, Gustavia   ☎ 590-27-61-63
Maurice Questel, Airport   ☎ 590-27-73-22
Soleil Caraibe, Airport   ☎ 590-27-67-18
Guy Turb   ☎ 590-27-71-42
   (Airport & St. Barts Beach Hotel)
USA, Airport   ☎ 590-27-70-01

The ever-popular Mini-Moke gives you an island atmosphere!

Scooters & Motorcycles

Daredevils will find motorbikes, mopeds and scooters for rent, but you should be an experienced driver to tackle these winding roads. French law requires that a helmet be worn at all times. A motorbike or driver's license is required for rental, which averages about 140FF ($23) a day with a $100 deposit. In Gustavia, call Denis Dufau's **Rent Some Fun** (☎ 590-27-70-59), **Ernest Lédée** (☎ 590-27-61-63), **Frédéric Supligeau** (☎ 590-27-67-89) and **Ouanalao** (☎ 590-27-81-27) for rentals.

Guided Tours

Guided sightseeing tours are a good option for day trippers and first time St. Barts visitors. Three sightseeing itineraries have been created by the Office du Tourisme. All depart by minibus from the pier in front of the office on the Quai Général de Gaulle in Gustavia (☎ 27-87-27). The routes are:

◆ A 45-minute tour from Gustavia through Colombier, Flamands, Corossol and Public, returning to Gustavia with one stop. Cost: 150FF (about $25) for three people, 200 FF (about $33) for more than three persons.

◆ A one-hour excursion that departs Gustavia and goes through St. Jean, Salines, Grand Fond, Cul de Sac, Marigot and Lorient, returning to Gustavia. Two stops. Costs 200FF (about $33) for three people, 250FF (about $42) for over three people.

◆ A 1½-hour trip follows the one-hour tour itinerary and adds the villages of Colombier and Corossol. Three stops. Costs 250FF (about $42) for three, 300 FF (about $50) for more than three.

You can also design your own sightseeing itinerary.

Contact one of these tour operators for more information (dial 011 before number when calling from US; if dialing from on island just use last six digits):

Bruno Beal	☎ 590-27-60-05
Ren, Bernier	☎ 590-27-63-75
Jean Brin	☎ 590-27-63-90
Hugo Cagan	☎ 590-27-61-28

St. Barts

Céline Gréaux	☎ 590-27-65-98
Emile Gréaux	☎ 590-27-66-01
Raymond Gréaux	☎ 590-27-66-32
Rémy Gréaux	☎ 590-27-63-60
Florian Laplace	☎ 590-27-63-58
Marie-Claude Lédée	☎ 590-27-60-54
Robert Magras	☎ 590-27-63-12

Beaches

 St. Barts is home to 22 beaches. All are topped with white sand and most are very quiet. Topless bathing is de rigueur here, although nudity is prohibited. Some top beaches include:

- ◆ Grand Cul de Sac, northeast shore. Watersports, restaurants and hotels nearby.

- ◆ Flamands, west. A beautiful beach fringed with lantana palms.

- ◆ Marigot, north. Very private

- ◆ Lorient, north. Very private.

- ◆ Gouverneur, south. Private.

- ◆ Shell Beach, Gustavia. Covered with small shells instead of sand. Pretty cliffs here and a relaxed atmosphere just steps from town.

Adventures

On Foot

Beachcombing

 Shell Beach in Gustavia is great for beachcombing. True to its name, the beach is covered with small shells, each almost identical in shape and size. Pretty cliffs.

On Wheels

Mountain Biking

Mountain bikes are available for those up to the challenge of steep roads. Look for 18-speed mountain bikes at Denis Dufau's **Rent Some Fun** (☎ 590-27-70-59) in Gustavia.

On Water

Scuba Diving

Scuba divers find plenty of good sites around the island, including **Pain de Sucre,** an islet off the Gustavia harbor. Trips cost about 250FF ($42) per person including gear. Dive operators include **Marine Service**, Gustavia (☎ 590-27-70-34), offering night dives; **St. Barth Plongée**, also in Gustavia (☎ 590-27-54-44), PADI operation; **Ocean Must** (☎ 590-27-62-25) in La Pointe; **Rainbow Dive Boat** (☎ 590-27-91-79), offering a 33-foot boat with US gear, near Wall House in Gustavia; and **Scuba Club la Bulle** (☎ 590-27-68-93) in St. Jean.

Snorkeling

Good snorkel spots are found throughout the island, especially on the leeward (western) side. Most hotels offer rental gear or rent through **Marine Service** (☎ 590-27-70-34) in Gustavia.

Island Hopping

Explore neighboring St. Martin with a quick trip aboard the *Voyager 2*, which departs from Gustavia to Marigot, St. Martin at 7:15 a.m. and 4 p.m. daily (reservations required for Sunday departure). The hour-and-a-half trip aboard the high-speed boat is comfortable, air-conditioned and includes a stocked bar. Round-trip is $50 plus a $9 tax. For reservations for information, call Corine or Philip at ☎ 590-87-20-28 or fax 590-87-20-78.

Yachting

St. Barts is a favorite stop with yachties. Located halfway between Antigua and Virgin Gorda, it's a natural stop over. Gustavia's harbor is 13 to 16 feet deep and has mooring and docking facilities for about 40 yachts, although it estimates it could take 500 yachts at anchor. Anchorages are also available at Public, Corossol and Colombier.

The yachting calendar is filled with annual events such as **St. Barth Regatta** just before Lent; the **Saint Barth's Cup** in April, sponsored by the Saint Barth Yacht Club; and the three-day **International Regatta** in May, with races for gaffers, cruising, etc.

Sailing

Those without their own vessel will find bareboat rentals as well as one-day and sunset cruises available. Full-day sails usually depart Gustavia for the Ile Fourchue and a morning of swimming, snorkeling, cocktails and gourmet lunch with wine, then make an afternoon stop at the Bay of Colombier. Full-day cruises cost about $96 per person; half-day cruises with swimming, snorkeling and open bar run about $52 per person.

For more on the various sailing options, contact **Nautica F.W.I.** (☎ 590-27-56-50), **Marine Service** (☎ 590-27-70-34) or **Ocean Must** (☎ 27-62-25), a company that operates the Ttoko-Ttoko 46-foot catamaran with half-and full-day sails and snorkel cruises.

Deep-Sea Fishing

Try your luck angling for tuna, bonito, dorado, marlin, wahoo or barracuda in the waters north of Lorient, Flamands and Corossol. Charter boats are available on a full-day or half-day basis. Costs run about 4,000 FF ($665) for a full day with meals and drinks or 2,500 FF ($420) for a half-day with drinks only. Fishing gear for four is included in the fare.

For **charter fishing boats**, contact **Marine Service** (☎ 590-27-70-34) or **Ocean Must** (☎ 590-27-62-25).

Windsurfing

St. Jean, Grand Cul de Sac, Flamands, and **Lorient** are top wind-surfing spots, although experts prefer the coast between Toiny and Grand Fond. Rentals average about $15-$18 per hour and lessons are available. Contact these operators for more information: **St. Barth Wind School** (☎ 590-27-71-22) at St. Jean, **Wind Wave Power** (☎ 590-27-62-73) in Grand Cul de Sac and **Ouanalao** (☎ 590-27-81-27) in Gustavia.

Watersports are prohibited in the Gustavia harbor.

Bodysurfing

Bodysurfers can test their skills at a site dubbed the "**washing machine**" by islanders. Located on the southeast coast, access to this area is by sea or with a 10-minute walk from Grand Fond Beach along Chemin Douanier. Another good site is **Anse de Lorient** on the north coast, **Anse Toiny** (both surfing and bodysurfing) on the southwest coast (although swimming is not recommended here due to strong currents.)

On Horseback

Ranch des Flamands offers horseback rides on trails throughout the island. The stables contain 15 horses and activities are available on the ranch as well, including jumping in the arena and horse ball. Beginners are welcome as well. For information, ☎ 011-590-27-80-72.

Eco-Travel

St. Barth Adventures (☎ 011-590-27-50-79) offers "mild to wild" guided tours, including kayaking, hiking and snorkeling. Options include the out islands, a 30-minute walk to Secret Beach, caves, cliff diving and more. Most tours are limited to four people.

Sightseeing

Day trippers enter the harbor town of **Gustavia** at the waterfront, within easy walking distance of its fine shops and sidewalk cafés. Filled with delicious French atmosphere, this small town can sometimes be bustling, with streams of traffic.

The town is built on a U-shape, following the harbor. On one side lies the tourist office, duty-free shops and several cafés; on the other side lie many good restaurants and the Musée de St. Barthélemy.

Gustavia's harbor.

Musée de St. Barthélemy, Gustavia, (☎ 011-590-27-87-27). This small museum is situated in the Wall House on the far side of the harbor. Exhibits explain more about the island's history through old photos, paintings and documents.

The museum is open Monday through Thursday, 8:30 to 12:30 and 2:30-6, Friday 3 to 6 and Saturday, 9 - 11. Admission is 10FF (about $2).

The two small towns (300 residents each) of **Colombier** and **Corossol** (northwest of Gustavia) are home to a population of older women who wear the traditional dress of the French provincial regions of Brittany, Normandy and Poitou. Long-sleeved dresses and sun bonnets called *calaches* or *quichonettes*. They are usually barefoot or wearing sandals. Most produce straw hats and baskets for the tourist market and requests for photos are rarely granted.

Inter-Oceans Museum, Corossol. This collection of 7,000 seashells is worth a visit. Admission is 20FF (about $4).

Shell Beach, Gustavia. Located just over the hill from town, this beach is worth a visit even if you don't want to swim.

Where to Stay

 There is no hotel tax on St. Barts. Most properties charge a 5-15% service charge, others include it in the quoted rate.

Hotels & Resorts

Carl Gustaf, ☎ 800-9-GUSTAF. $$$+. Overlooking Gustavia, this hotel offers 14 suites, each with a Jacuzzi plunge pool and private sun deck. The hotel has a fitness center and is just a short walk from the beach. The views by day or night are incredible. Each suite includes a stereo system, fax, cable TV with English- and French-language programming, kitchen facilities, air-conditioning and ceiling fan. The hotel is 500 feet from a white sand beach and a 48-foot yacht is available for island hopping, snorkel trips or deep-sea fishing.

The Carl Gustaf overlooks Gustavia.

The Christopher Hotel, ☎ 800-763-4835. $$$. This 40-room hotel (all with ocean views) is on Pointe Milou in the northeastern part of St. Barts, about a 10-minute drive from the airport and 15 minutes from Gustavia. All rooms have ceiling fans, private terrace and hairdryers. The hotel restaurant serves French cuisine and offers a prix fixe gourmet dinner plan. Facilities include a swim-

St. Barts

ming pool and the hotel staff can arrange scuba diving, snorkeling, deep-sea fishing, horseback riding and other activities.

Eden Rock, ☎ (011-590-27-72-94). $$$. This was St. Barts' first hotel and is still one of its most photographed. Perched on St. Jean Bay between two white sand beaches, Eden Rock was built in the 1950s and was recently renovated and enlarged.

Hotel Guanahani, ☎ 800-932-3222. $$$. Très chic, this full-service resort consists of 75 West Indian style cottages, each brightly colored and overlooking the sea. Guanahani is the Arawak name for San Salvador, the first island discovered by Christopher Columbus. Set on a 16-acre peninsula on the northeastern side of the island, the hotel offers two tennis courts lit for night play (a tennis pro is also on hand if you want to improve your game). It has two freshwater pools and a heated Jacuzzi, but it's hard for pools to compete with Guanahani's two beaches. Here, guests can go snorkeling, sail a Hobie Cat, windsurf or go deep-sea fishing. One beach is on a quiet lagoon and the other at the edge of a coconut grove facing the ocean. Complimentary continental breakfast is included as well as round-trip airport transfers, service charge and tax.

Sea Horse Hotel, ☎ 800-223-9832. $$. A good bargain on a high-priced island, the Sea Horse Hotel has 10 suites and one two-bedroom villa. The units overlook Marigot Bay and each has an air-conditioned bedroom, living room, kitchenette and a covered terrace.

Villas

St. Barts has many villas and apartments for rent by the week or by the month. One-week winter rates range from $1,200 to $1,800 for a one-bedroom, one-bath bungalow to $4,500-$10,000 for a four-bedroom villa with pool. During the summer months, rates fall 25-40%. Expect to pay about $40 per person per day for catered meals or $15 per hour for a cook. Rental agencies include:

Ici et Là	☎ 011-590-27-78-78
Sibarth Real Estate	☎ 011-590-27-62-38

Where to Eat

 Dining is as much an adventure on St. Barts as watersports or hiking. An activity that's the deciding factor for many vacationers, the fine dining found here often features French cuisine, so much so that the island has earned a reputation as the "French cuisine capital of the Caribbean." Expect these meals to set you back at least $50 per person in most cases and sometimes much more.

Since a meal is more than just food but close to an investment, you might do a little research beforehand. Stop by the Tourist Office in Gustavia for restaurant brochures and a copy of *Ti Gourmet*, a free guide that includes several bonus coupons. Another source is **Sibarth** (☎ 011-590-27-62-38), a villa rental company on rue Général de Gaulle in Gustavia. The offices have menus from most island restaurants.

American

Cheeseburger in Paradise, Gustavia, ☎ 590-27-86-87, $-$$. Named for St. Barts regular Jimmy Buffett, this casual eatery sits in a garden right in the heart of Gustavia. A favorite with yachties, it's a fun place to grab a brew and a burger and watch the parade of activity in town.

French

Carl Gustaf, rue des Normands, Gustavia, ☎ 590-27-82-83, $$$. Fine food served in a beautiful atmosphere brings diners to Carl Gustaf for a memorable meal. Typical dishes include Caribbean lobster tail and green papaya salad, Oriental prawn risotto, fricassée of shellfish with fresh pasta, noisettes of monkfish seasoned with herbs or breast of duck served in its own juices. Entrées range from $25-$50 each (even the soup is $16) so bring the bucks for a dinner here. If you can't spare that kind of change, drop by the piano bar for a drink and a spectacular sunset.

Francois Plantation, Colombier, ☎ 590-27-78-82, $$$. This terraced restaurant serves lobster gazpacho, cold or hot foie gras, Jamaican roasted tournedos of ostrich in cajun spices, jumbo shrimp sautéed with citronella and ginger and more. Save room for one of the desserts: crème brûlée flavored with candied ginger and lime or banana and coconut tarte tatin. An extensive wine list is also available. Open for dinner only.

Hotel Le Toiny's Restaurant Le Gaiac, Anse le Toiny, ☎ 590-27-88-88, $$$. Situated in the main house of Hotel Le Toiny, this restaurant is named for the rare gaiac trees found on the property. Gourmet dishes include cold caviar soup with anise and beetroot, medallions of lobster with a passion fruit vinaigrette and candied sweet peppers, gâteau of roast boneless pigeon layered with red cabbage and sweet potato – and more. Stop by on Sunday afternoons for a poolside buffet luncheon.

Le Paradisio, rue du Roi Oscar II, Gustavia, ☎ 590-27-80-78, $$-$$$. With indoor and outdoor dining in a garden terrace, this restaurant offers a good list of French wines followed by dishes such as squid creole on a bed of macaroni, mahi mahi with creole sauce, filet mignon with grey pepper sauce or pink salmon over French lentils.

Le Sapotillier, rue du Centenaire, Gustavia, ☎ 590-27-60-28, $$$. Dine outside beneath an old sapodilla tree or in the dining room at this downtown restaurant open for dinner only. Dishes include pan fired Dover sole, cocotte of fishes with anise flavoring or filet of duck. Save room for the crème brûlée.

Restaurant le Bistrot des Arts, rue Jeanne d'Arc (far side of harbor), Gustavia, ☎ 590-27-70-00, $$-$$$. Decorated with artwork, this bistro offers up pizzas prepared in the brick oven, including a pizza à la creole with pineapple, spicy West Indian sausage and crab. Parisian onion soup, Caribbean fish soup and other specialties are served as well. This restaurant boasts a good view of the harbor and the downtown, but service can be glacial.

St. Kitts & Nevis

They're often referred to as "the way the Caribbean used to be before WWII." Life is quiet and unspoiled on this two-island nation where most guests stay in small, locally owned plantation inns that recall the heritage of the Caribbean with period antiques, wide porches to pick up gentle trade winds and an atmosphere that appeals to independent travelers ready to strike out on their own.

Rugged and tropical, both islands are excellent destinations for hikers, birders and nature lovers. **St. Kitts** is the largest of the two, spanning 68 square miles. The island is 23 miles long and, at its widest point, five miles across. St. Kitts offers varying terrains that range from semi-arid to rainforest, from flat to mountainous. Most of the population lives on St. Kitts with a large percentage in the capital city of **Basseterre** (pronounced bos-tear). Throughout the island, modern life and ancient history live hand-in-hand. The island is sprinkled with historic sites that date back both to pre-history and to the days of colonization.

Basseterre on a beautiful Caribbean day.

Development has, thankfully, been slow on St. Kitts. Although the island has one all-inclusive property, most hotels are locally owned and managed and provide a genuine Caribbean experience. They're found sprinkled throughout the island, both at seaside destinations and high in the hills overlooking fields that were formerly part of plantations.

The most noticeable feature of St. Kitts is **Mount Liamuiga** (pronounced Lee-a-MWEEGA), usually fringed with a ring of clouds. This dormant volcano, elevation 3,792 feet, is home to the island's tropical rainforest and an excellent destination for eco-travelers. Guided tours (see *Adventures on Foot*, below) take visitors to the far reaches of the forest for a look at this ecosystem.

One area presently being eyed for development is the Southeast Peninsula, a site that, until a few years ago, could be reached only by boat. Since the days when the British and the French fought for domination of St. Kitts, the Southeast Peninsula has remained impenetrable. Although it was blessed with white sand beaches and palm-fringed coves, this rugged area was inhabited only by troupes of green vervet monkeys and shy white-tailed deer, along with a few die-hard residents who traveled by boat.

But then along came the U.S. military. Soon they accomplished what others had tried to do but failed: to complete the Dr. Kennedy Simmonds Highway. The $14 million road now links this final frontier with the rest of the Caribbean island.

Just two miles away from St. Kitts lies the tiny island of **Nevis** (pronounced NEE-vis), covering a total of 36 square miles. Columbus first named this island because of the ever-present cloud that circled Mount Nevis, giving it almost a snow-capped look ("nieves" means snow). Today, the cloud still lingers over the mountain peak. Home to only 9,000 residents, this country cousin has a charming atmosphere all its own, plus a good share of plantation houses where guests can enjoy a look back at Caribbean history.

Eco-tourism is a major draw on Nevis. **Mount Nevis** offers many hikes of varying difficulty levels. History buffs find numerous sites of interest in the capital city of **Charlestown**. Like its sister island, Nevis is home to many vervet monkeys, a reminder of the French occupation of the island centuries ago. When the British took over the island from the French, they didn't mind transporting their enemies back home, but they weren't about to send their favorite pets with them. Small vervet monkeys had been imported from

Africa by the French. The British turned the monkeys loose on the island, where they prospered. Today, it's estimated that the monkeys of St. Kitts and Nevis outnumber humans two-to-one. If you get up early or go out after sunset, you'll stand a chance of spotting one of the primates.

St. Kitts & Nevis recognize the value of their environmental resources and have declared that, by law, no building may be taller than a palm tree.

The solitude and privacy offered on both islands attract a celebrity clientele. In recent years, the islands have been chosen as a getaway for Princess Diana, Oprah Winfrey, Sylvester Stallone, Danny Glover, Robert De Niro and Michael J. Fox, among others.

History

The story of St. Kitts and Nevis began long before European discovery. The islands' first settlers were the Caribs, a fierce people known for their cannibalism. It wasn't until 1493, on his second voyage to the New World, that Columbus spotted the islands. The larger he first named San Jorge and then renamed St. Christopher for the patron saint of travelers, a name it retains today (St. Kitts is a nickname given to the isle by the British). Columbus first named the smaller island San Martin, but later renamed it Nuestro Señora de las Nieves, Our Lady of the Snows, because of the ever-present cloud that circled Mount Nevis and gave it almost a snow-capped look. Lush rainforest lies beneath its shadows.

All remained quiet on these islands until 1623 when the British arrived to colonize St. Kitts. Just a couple of years later, a French ship, looking for a port after a fight with a Spanish galleon, arrived on the island and the two joined forces to annihilate the Carib Indians. Later, the French and English worked together to quell a Spanish attack. The English set about colonizing nearby islands – Antigua, Barbuda and Montserrat – while the French claimed Martinique and Guadeloupe. But the peace between the British and French was not to last. Skirmishes began by the mid-1600s. For decades, the British and the French fought over St. Kitts, so much, in fact, that the English finally built one of the largest forts in the islands. Brimstone Hill, nicknamed the "Gibraltar of the Caribbean," guarded the island from a point over 400 feet above sea level. Apparently it didn't protect the shoreline well enough, how-

St. Kitts & Nevis

ever, because in 1782 the French captured the fortress and ruled the island. The next year the tables turned and the losers were loaded onto British ships and sent back to the old country. In 1690, tiny Nevis was hit by a massive earthquake. A resulting tidal wave destroyed the capital city of Jamestown and sunk part of the island.

Throughout these years, a plantation system was found throughout both islands. Nevis was the slave market for many neighboring islands as the headquarters for the Royal African Company from 1600-1698. A century later, over 10,000 slaves worked the tobacco and cane fields of the island. Over 50 sugar plantations operated on St. Kitts, using sail-driven windmills to grind the sugarcane. Not until 1833 was slavery abolished in all British colonies; today the first Monday in August is still celebrated as Emancipation Day.

The estate plantation system grew less and less important around the island as technology developed. Wind-driven power gave way to steam power. In 1912, the sugar railroad was constructed around the island of St. Kitts, soon making the factories on the individual estates obsolete.

As social changes occurred in the island, so did political ones. In 1871, St. Kitts was placed in a federation with Anguilla and soon Nevis was added. The relationship between the islands was always a tumultuous one, with claims from Anguilla that St. Kitts ignored the much smaller isle in terms of representation and aid. The ill feelings rose in intensity until 1967 when the Anguilla rebellion brought about independence from St. Kitts.

The rebellion caught the attention of the world and the tiny island was given the nickname "The Mouse that Roared." St. Kitts and Nevis remain a part of the British Commonwealth and the Queen is represented by a Governor-General on St. Kitts with a Deputy Governor-General stationed on Nevis. On September 19, 1983, Nevis and St. Kitts became an independent state with a Prime Minister and House of Assembly. At press time, an election on Nevis voted for secession from St. Kitts.

TIMELINE

1493 First recorded sighting by Columbus.

1623 British arrived to colonize St. Kitts.

1642 Population of Nevis was 10,000.

1690 Nevis was hit by a massive earthquake.

1782 French captured Brimstone Hill fortress and ruled the island.

1787 Admiral Horatio Nelson married Nevisian Fanny Nisbet at Montpelier.

1793 British took over St. Kitts.

1833 Slavery abolished in all British colonies.

1871 St. Kitts was placed in a federation with Anguilla and soon Nevis was added.

1929 Charles Lindberg carried the first recorded mails to St. Kitts and Nevis. Two years and four months after his trans-Atlantic crossing, the aviator touched down at Pinney's Beach.

1967 Anguilla rebellion. St. Kitts and Nevis lost the third island in the federation.

1983 Nevis and St. Kitts became an independent state.

1998 St. Kitts & Nevis will most likely become two countries.

Geography & Land

St. Kitts is a volcanic island of about 68 square miles. Shaped like a guitar or paddle, the most noticeable feature of the island is **Mt. Liamuiga** (until 1983 named Mt. Misery – not a good addition to the tourist brochures). The volcano has long been dormant.

Only 35 miles square, Nevis is a small link in the Caribbean chain but it packs plenty of beauty into its diminutive size. The circular island rises from the sea to the top of **Nevis Peak** at 3,232 feet above sea level. Steep mountainsides are dotted with coconut palms that wind all the way down to the water's edge. Only one road circles Mount Nevis and the island, winding from the capital city of **Charlestown** to communities such as St. George and Newcastle,

St. Kitts & Nevis

passing plantations that lie in ruin and others which have been renovated and now serve as charming bed and breakfasts.

Climate

St. Kitts and Nevis enjoy an average temperature of 79°. Mean rainfall is 55 inches (but higher in the rainforest areas).

Flora & Fauna

Plant Life

The plant life found on both St. Kitts and Nevis is bountiful and beautiful, thanks to frequent rains. Vegetation grows thickest in the rainforest areas of both islands, but you'll see a variety of species anywhere you go. You'll find: bamboo; wild coffee; seagrape; wild cherries; wild sage; flamboyant (the national flower of St. Kitts and Nevis, these trees bloom with brilliant red flowers in the winter months); breadfruit, first brought to the islands by Captain Cook and now a staple of island diets, used much like a potato; mango; silk cotton tree; screw pine; soursop.

And if you think you see pineapples growing on the islands, you're right. A new variety of high-sugar-content pineapples has been introduced to St. Kitts and Nevis by agriculturists from the Republic of China. Tainung No. 4 and Kain varieties, which usually obtain about six pounds in China, reach 8½ pounds on these tropical isles. One explanation of the fruit's success is the pure water found on both islands and the fertile soil.

Animals

The best known resident of St. Kitts and Nevis is the **African green (vervet) monkey**, a reminder of the French occupation of the island centuries ago. The French brought the monkeys here from Africa as pets, but today the animals have thrived in the lush forests of St. Kitts and Nevis, outnumbering the human population two-to-one.

They're both the delight of visitors and the bane of residents, with raids on fruit trees by the wily monkeys. The monkeys do not have a prehensile tail, so they're often seen on the ground, scampering across a lawn in search of a fallen mango. Social like other monkeys, the green monkeys often travel in groups of 30 or 40.

Early mornings and late evenings are the best times to spot this common resident. Come out at sunset and sunrise for the best chance to view the vervet monkeys. Look in the underbrush and not in the trees.

A wide-eyed vervet monkey.
© St. Kitts & Nevis Tourist Board

Another mammal often spotted is the **mongoose**. Brought to the island from Jamaica, the mongoose was introduced to much of the Caribbean from India to control snakes in the sugarcane fields. Unfortunately, mongooses and rats don't keep the same schedule; the rats are sleeping while the mongooses are hunting. The mongooses have become somewhat of a pest on the island.

Far more beautiful residents are the **butterflies** of Nevis, often seen on Nevisian stamps as well as in the rainforest. The southern daggertail, the red rim, the mimic, the painted lady, the Caribbean buckeye, the flambeau, the tropical checkered skipper and many others in the *Nymphaelidae, Heliconiidae, Hesperiidae* and *Pieridae* families are spotted.

The tropical **honeybees** found on St. Kitts and Nevis are responsible for more than honey – they pollinate the thousands of blooms that make these islands so brilliant. Documented evidence of honeybees (*Apis mellifera*) on Nevis dates back to 1716 and it has long been a tradition for men to harvest the wild nests with a cutlass or

St. Kitts & Nevis

machete. Families used the honey for its medicinal properties, mixing it with lime to ease colds and sore throats.

Since the 1980s, beekeepers in Nevis have managed the bees in moveable frame hives, yielding 150 to 200 pounds of honey per hive every year. The bees are valued for their sweet product and for their role in pollinating sea grapes, coconuts, mangroves, mangos, sweet and sour oranges, genips and other local plants. The island has no Africanized honey bees and are protected from bee diseases found elsewhere because of the island's geographic isolation.

NEVIS HONEY

You can take home a taste of Nevis with honey sold at gift shops, museums and grocery stores around the island. Wholesale purchases can also be made from **The Nevis Beekeepers**, ☎ 869-469-5521, extension 2086. For more on this Nevisian industry, read *Beekeeping – The Nevis Way*, by J. Quentin Henderson, available at both the Horatio Nelson Museum and the Nevis Museum of History.

Government & Economy

St. Kitts and Nevis operate as an independent nation and a member of the British Commonwealth. Today much of the economy of St. Kitts and Nevis depends on tourism.

People & Culture

Much of the population traces its heritage back to African slaves first brought to these islands to work the sugar plantations. When slavery was outlawed, indentured laborers, many Portuguese, relocated here. Today, the population is 45,000 (9,000 of these residents are located on Nevis).

Travel Information

When to Go

St. Kitts and Nevis are good destinations any time of year. The atmosphere during winter months is somewhat dressier and more formal, however. During these months, an older, more affluent clientele frequents the islands, many from Britain. In low season (mid-April through mid-December), accommodation prices drop as much as 40% and the typical visitor is younger.

Customs

Passports are required of all visitors except US and Canadian citizens, who may present a voter's registration card, naturalization papers or a certified birth certificate (not a copy).

Cost

SAMPLE PRICE CHART

Bottled Coke (bottled on St. Kitts)	$1.00
Diet Coke (must be imported)	$1.50
Daily car rental	$50.00

Holidays

Public holidays include: New Year's Day, January 1; Carnival Last Lap, January 2; Good Friday; Easter Monday; Labour Day, May 5; Whit Monday, May 19; August Monday, August 5;

Culturama Last Lap, August 6; Independence Day, September 19; Christmas Day, December 25; Boxing Day, December 26.

These holidays just hint at the special events that take place throughout the calendar year on both St. Kitts and Nevis. During most holidays and festivals, Nevis comes to life with horse racing. Race days are scheduled during most special events and draw crowds for one of the Caribbean's most unique events.

CALENDAR OF EVENTS

◆ *January*

January 2nd Horse Races, **Nevis Alexander Hamilton Birthday Tea**, Nevis. Sponsored by the Nevis Island Administration, this event is held at the Museum of Nevis History, the birthplace of Alexander Hamilton.

Environmental Awareness Week, Nevis. Sponsored by the Nevis Historical and Conservation Society's Environmental Education Committee; ☎ 869-469-5786 for information.

◆ *February*

Nevis Tourism Week, Nevis. This eight-day celebration includes cultural expositions, watersports activities, horseracing, culinary contests and an arts and crafts exhibition. March Horse Racing, Special Nelson Memorial Race April Horse Racing, Easter Monday Earth Day, Nevis. Celebrated by the Nevis Historical and Conservation Society. May Horse Racing, May Day, Nevis.

International Museums Day, Nevis. Open houses are held at the Museum of Nevis History at Alexander Hamilton House in Charlestown and the Horatio Nelson Museum at Bellevue.

Flower Show, St. Kitts. Sponsored by the St. Kitts Horticultural Society, this annual show features local gardeners. Admission is $10 EC and includes refreshments. Rainforest tours are offered during the show for special rates.

◆ *May-June*
Leeward Island Cricket Tournament. For more information and dates, ☎ 869-469-5521.

◆ *June*
Sunfish & Windsurfing Regatta, St. Kitts and Nevis. This regional event includes 14-foot Sunfish and sailboards. The race spans the 11 miles from Frigate Bay, St. Kitts to Oualie Beach, Nevis. Food and music also make up the festivities.
Guavaberry Caribbean Offshore Regatta, St. Kitts. This competition spans from St. Maarten to Basseterre and includes food and music in he capital city.
World Environment Day. Sponsored by the Nevis Historical and Conservation Society.
Horseracing, **Whit Monday**, Nevis.
St. Kitts Music Festival, St. Kitts. This annual event draws both local and internationally known artists. Each night of the festival features a different type of music, from reggae and R&B to soca and gospel.

◆ *August*
Culturama, Nevis. This annual event celebrates the history, folklore and culture of the island.
Horseracing, Nevis. Scheduled for the first Monday in August, this special event commemorates the emancipation of slaves in the British West Indies.

◆ *September*
Independence Week Activities, St. Kitts and Nevis. Parades, picnics, dances and cocktail receptions celebrate the islands' independence.
Horseracing, **Independence Day**, Nevis.

◆ *October*
World Food Day, Nevis. Sponsored by the Nevis Historical and Conservation Society.
Oceanfest, St. Kitts. Windsurfers and Sunfish race from Nevis to St. Kitts. Other events include a fishing tournament, beach fête and music.

St. Kitts & Nevis

◆ *November*

Tourism Week, St. Kitts. A cultural program and watersports festival celebrate the tourism industry. Horseracing, **Thanksgiving**, Nevis.

◆ *December*

Carnival, St. Kitts. From Christmas Eve through January 3rd (pre-Carnival events begin two weeks earlier), the island parties with festivals, queen shows, calypso competitions, parades, street dances and more.
Horseracing, **Boxing Day**, Nevis.

Transportation

Air Service

Most visitors first arrive at St. Kitts' **Robert Llewelyn Bradshaw International Airport** (formerly Golden Rock Airport), with daily jet service from the US. American Airlines provides daily service from their Caribbean hub in San Juan. From the UK, service is available on British Airways, BWIA, Air France, Lufthansa and KLM through gateways in St. Maarten and Puerto Rico. From other Caribbean islands, service is available on BWIA, LIAT and Winair.

Air St. Kitts/Nevis, ☎ 809-469-9241; **Carib Aviation**, 809-465-3055; **LIAT**, 809-465-2286; **Nevis Express**, ☎ 869-469-9756; **Winair**, 869-465-4069 from St. Kitts, ☎ 869-469-5423 on Nevis.

FLIGHT TIMES: New York - 4 hours; Miami - 3 hours; London -8 hours; Antigua - 20 minutes; Puerto Rico - 1 hour; St. Maarten - 20 minutes. From St. Kitts, air service to Nevis' small Newcastle Airport is offered by commuter flights from St. Kitts. Air St. Kitts and Nevis Express whisk visitors from island to island in less than 10 minutes.

Cruise Ship Terminal

St. Kitts' new $16.25 million cruise ship terminal is located in **Basseterre**. Visitors arrive just off Pelican Mall, a new establishment with 26 shops that feature tropical clothing, locally made goods and tourist items. Kittitian architecture makes this mall different from the typical mall you might see back home.

Nevis is presently constructing a new cruise port in **Charlestown**.

Ferry Port

To reach Nevis, most people travel by ferry. Service is available several times daily aboard *The Caribe Queen*; the journey takes 45 minutes and costs $20EC (about US $8) round-trip. Departure is from Basseterre, St. Kitts and arrival is in Charlestown, Nevis.

CARIBE QUEEN SCHEDULE

	Depart Nevis	Depart St. Kitts
Monday	7.00 a.m.	8:00 a.m.
	3:00 p.m.	4:00 p.m.
Tuesday	7:30 a.m.	1:00 p.m.
	6:00 p.m.	-
Wednesday	-	7: 00 a.m.
	-	8:00 a.m.
	-	4:00 p.m.
	-	6:00 p.m.
	-	7:00 p.m.
Thursday	No Departures	
Friday	No Departures	
Saturday	7:30 a.m.	8:30 a.m.
	2:00 p.m.	3:00 p.m.
Sunday	No Departures	

When leaving St. Kitts and Nevis (but not to travel between the islands), visitors pay a departure tax of $27 EC.

St. Kitts & Nevis

Special Concerns

Currency

The Eastern Caribbean dollar (EC) is used throughout St. Kitts and Nevis. The fixed exchange rate is US$1 = EC$2.68.

Electricity

230 volts, 60 cycles. Most hotels have 110 volts and converters are available.

Medical Facilities

Both St. Kitts and Nevis has doctors on call at hotels. Recompression chambers are available by air ambulance at nearby Saba and in St. Thomas.

Dress

Swimsuits may be the uniform of the beach, but wear a cover-up away from the sand and swimming pool. Both St. Kitts and Nevis are a little dressier than some of the other Caribbean islands, especially during high season. You'll feel comfortable at dinner in casually elegant wear (jackets are optional for men at most establishments, and don't worry about a tie).

Nude and topless sunbathing is prohibited throughout St. Kitts and Nevis.

Crime

Crime is rare in both St. Kitts and Nevis. However, no destination is completely crime-free. Use the same common-sense precautions you would exercise at home. Also, don't leave items unattended while you're at the beach; lock items in your car or leave them in your hotel room.

Drugs

St. Kitts and Nevis exercise strict anti-drug laws. Marijuana is an illegal substance and possession of it can result not only in large fines but also in a prison term.

Tipping

Leave 10% to 15%, depending on the service. Some restaurants and hotels will automatically add a 10% gratuity. Porters and bellhops usually tipped 50¢ US per bag; taxi drivers are tipped 10 to 15% of the total fare.

Weddings

Getting married on St. Kitts or Nevis is a simple feat. Either the bride or groom must be a resident of the island for 48 hours prior to the wedding. Bring along a valid passport or certified birth certificate and, if either party is divorced, present an absolute decree of divorce. If either the bride or groom is widowed, a death certificate is necessary. (If the documents are not in English, a notarized translation must be presented.) To be married by a Catholic priest, you must bring a letter from your resident priest verifying that you are unmarried and have received necessary instruction. To be married by an Anglican minister, bring a letter from your minister verifying that you are unmarried. The marriage license fee is $200 EC (or $80 US). If you have been on St. Kitts or Nevis for at least 15 days prior to the marriage, the fee goes down to $50 EC or $20 US.

Sources of Information

For brochures and maps of the islands, contact the **St. Kitts and Nevis Tourism Office**, 414 East 75th St., New York, NY 10021, ☎ 800-582-6208 or 212-535-1234. Fax your information request to 212-734-6511 or e-mail skbnev@ix.netcom.com In Canada, contact the **Tourism Office** at 365 Bay Street, Suite 806, Toronto, Ontario M5H2V1, ☎ 416-368-6707 or fax 416-368-3934. While on St. Kitts, stop by the Basseterre office on the first floor of Pelican Mall for assistance, brochures and maps. In Nevis, the tourism office is located in Charlestown. An excellent source of St. Kitts and Nevis information is the Web page for the islands, accessible at http://www.interknowlege.com/stkitts-nevis.

St. Kitts & Nevis

St. Kitts

Out on the Island

St. Kitts is shaped somewhat like a guitar – or, to be less glamorous, a chicken drumstick. The skinny stretch is the **Southeast Peninsula**, a region that's largely undeveloped (at least for now; plans are in the works for a major hotel to make its home on these pristine beaches) and the perfect place for birdwatching, monkey spotting and strolling beaches with no sign of human life. Birders find the Great Salt Pond, Little Salt Pond and Majors Bay Pond all good sites.

The Southeast Peninsula meets the main part of the island at steep **Sir Timothy's Hill**. On each side of this steep hill (which is flanked by an excellent scenic overlook to pull over and get a good view of both the Caribbean and the Atlantic at the same time) lies **Frigate Bay**. North Frigate Bay is on the Caribbean side, while Frigate Bay lies on the Atlantic side. On this stretch of the island are many hotel accommodations and guest services and much of the watersports activities.

Market vendor in Basseterre.

The road turns left to **Basseterre**, the capital of St. Kitts. This charming waterfront community bustles with activity on market days and is home to many buildings constructed in traditional West Indian style.

From Basseterre, the main road travels northwest through many small communities and over many ghuts, natural draws from which heavy rains can run off Mt. Liamuiga and into the sea. The road skirts the mountain and hugs the coastline with turnoffs for attractions such as Romney Manor, the home of a batik factory and some beautiful grounds at the edge of the rainforest and the Carib petroglyphs.

About two-thirds up the island is the turn for **Brimstone Hill Fortress**, one of the most formidable structures in the Caribbean and a mandatory stop on any island tour.

On the north side of the island lies Rawlins Plantation and the Golden Lemon, a former plantation with a beautiful black sand volcanic beach. In this part of St. Kitts, long vistas across acres of crops are common sights.

On the east side of the island the views are often of the Caribbean Sea. Here Ottley's Plantation Inn draws visitors and offers sweeping vistas across historic grounds that back up to the rainforest.

A unique sight in St. Kitts is the **Sugar Train**, a narrow gauge railroad. A small engine pulls the open-air cars through the fields of sugar cane, picking up the harvest and eventually delivering it to the factory in Needsmust. Look out in the fields as you exit Bradshaw International Airport for a peek at the train; it's also visible in the fields at several points around the island.

Getting Around

Rental Cars & Taxi Service

Getting around St. Kitts can be accomplished by taxi or rental car, depending on your independence and the frequency with which you wish to travel around the island. If you think you'll be journeying down to the Southeast Peninsula and buzzing around the island beyond an island tour, it's worth it to rent a car for your stay. Rentals are readily available (see below).

Taxi rates are set, although these can change. Within Basseterre, you can journey from one point to another for $3 US, with the charge of $1 for every 15 minutes waiting period after the first 15 minutes and 50¢ for each additional piece of luggage beyond two. Rates increase between the hours of 11 p.m. and 6 a.m.

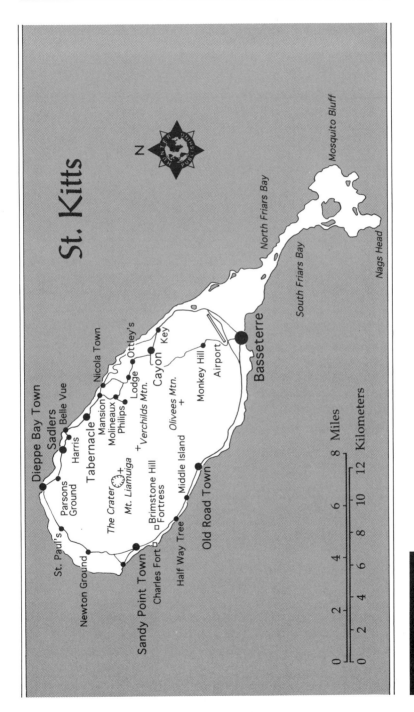

St. Kitts

TAXI RATES

From Airport to Basseterre	$5
From airport to Frigate Bay	$10
From airport to Ottleys	$9
From Basseterre to Turtle Bay, round-trip	$32
Taxi tour to Brimstone Hill	$32
Taxi tour to Brimstone Hill and Caribelle Batik	$42
Taxi tour of Southeast Peninsula from Jack Tar	$20
Island taxi tour from Basseterre	$49
Island taxi tour from Jack Tar	$49

Car Rental Companies

Driving on St. Kitts requires a temporary driver's license, which costs $30 EC. The license is valid for one year and can be obtained from the Police Traffic Department.

Driving in St. Kitts and Nevis is on the **left**. Rental car rates run about $55 EC per day for a mid-size car.

Caines Rent-A-Car	☎ 869-456-2366
Choice Car Rental	☎ 869-465-4422
Delisle Walwyn Car Rental	☎ 869-465-8449
Holiday Car Rental	☎ 869-465-6507
Higgins Car Rental	☎ 869-465-8080
Island Car Rental	☎ 869-465-3000
Kitts Car Rental	☎ 869-465-1665
St. Kitts Taxi Association	☎ 869-465-4253/8487
Sunshine Car Rental	☎ 869-465-2193
TDC Rentals Ltd.	☎ 869-465-2991

Airport

St. Kitts' **Robert L. Bradshaw International Airport** has undergone a $46 million extension and improvement. The arrival hall has doubled its capacity and includes enhanced Customs & Immigration areas. Also, lifts for the disabled have been added. Nevis is also enlarging its airport, expanding its airstrip to accommodate larger planes.

Guided Tours

Guided island tours are a good way for first time visitors to enjoy an overview of the islands. You can hire a taxi driver for a personalized tour or call one of these tour companies:

Kris Fix It and Tours, ☎ 869-465-4042; **TDC Tours**, ☎ 869-465-5978; **Tropical Tours**, ☎ 869-465-4767.

Tours depart by ferry from St. Kitts for island tours of Nevis including the Bath Hotel, Government House, St. John's Anglican House and plantation inns.

Additional tours are available for hikers and walkers; see *Adventures On Foot*, below.

Adventures

On Foot

With its towering volcano, lush rainforests and beautiful beaches, St. Kitts offers a plethora of hikes to satisfy any visitor. Strike out on your own for a quiet stroll or with a guide for a look at more out-of-the-way areas of the island.

Guided Hikes

Guided tours of the rainforest are a popular option, most combining a guided ride with a hike. Rainforest and volcano tours are available from several operators:

Greg's Safaris (PO Box 65, Basseterre, St. Kitts, West Indies, ☎ 869-465-4121 or 465-5209; fax 869-465-1057) offers a half-day guided Rainforest Safari through mountain trails into the Oceanic Rainforest. Visitors have a chance to look for bird life, cross springs, identify exotic wildflowers and enjoy the mist-shrouded forest.

Greg's Safari's also runs a full-day Volcano Safari. This strenuous trip includes a rugged hike up the volcano to view the mile-wide crater rim and a chance to see the cloud forest and steaming sulphur vents in the volcanic region. The hike is a tough one, so come prepared with very good walking shoes.

Kriss Tours (☎ 869-465-4042) offers half- and full-day tours of the rainforest and, on the full-day tour, of the volcanic rim.

Tropical Tours (☎ 869-465-4167) offers a St. Kitts island tour, half-day rainforest tour, cave explorer tour and volcano crater tour.

Scenic Walks

One scenic walk is to a lookout site called **Black Rocks** near Belle Vue. This seaside attraction is made of lava that flowed from Mt. Liamuiga and cooled when it reached the water, forming interesting shapes.

Tread carefully here as the cliffs are steep and occasionally the winds can be fierce along this shoreline.

A far more strenuous hike is to the crater rim of **Mt. Liamuiga**, an all-day excursion only for those ready for a challenge.

Admire the view at Black Rocks.

On Water

Scuba Diving

St. Kitts is fairly new to the diving scene and offers divers a world of pristine sites without crowds. The most popular dive sites are found on the western side of the island in the calmer Caribbean waters. Here, visibility runs up to 100 feet. Some top dive spots include:

> **Black Coral Reef.** This dive site is located from 40 to 70 feet below the surface and is best known for its protected black coral.

Bloody Bay Reef. At 60 to 80 feet, this dive site is noted for its healthy undersea life, from anemones to sea fans. A popular fishing site as well, an occasional shark is seen here, the result of chumming. Divers will find several caves in this area.

The Caves. Just off the coast of Charlestown lies this undersea adventure, a series of coral grottos that invite exploration. Marine life is plentiful along this shallow 40-foot dive and divers usually spot plenty of squirrel fish, lobster, sponges and an array of corals.

Coconut Tree Reef. A variety of dive experiences, from beginner to advanced, are available on this reef, which starts at 40 feet below the surface before plunging to over 200 feet. Beautiful corals and bountiful marine life are found here.

Grid Iron. Found in the channel between St. Kitts and Nevis, this dive follows an undersea shelf. Look for angelfish as well as rich aquatic life on this dive.

Monkey Reef. You won't see any monkeys down here, but plenty of other life awaits: nurse sharks, stingrays, lobster and more. This is a shallow dive, approximately 50 feet below the surface off the Southeast Peninsula.

Nags Head. This advanced dive is found where the calm Caribbean Sea meets the more rugged waters of the Atlantic Ocean. The result is a strong current and rich marine life, including rays and turtles. This dive averages about 80 feet below the sea.

Booby Island. Situated in the St. Kitts and Nevis channel called "The Narrows," Booby Island is for advanced divers only because of the strong current. Jacks and snapper are common here.

Sandy Point Bay. Over 50 anchors and marine artifacts have been spotted at a section of this site nicknamed "Anchors Away." On other parts of the dive, large basket sponges, jacks and snappers are spotted.

Wreck Diving

As rich as St. Kitts' dive sites are, her wreck sites also attract many divers. The waters around the islands are dotted with wrecks and estimates are that 390 ships sunk off the coast between 1492 and 1825. Some favorites include:

River Taw. This 144-foot freighter was sunk about a decade ago and sits just 50 feet below the surface, making it a favorite destination for beginners. It is encrusted with corals and is home to many reef fish.

M.V. Talata. Sunk in 1985, this freighter is still in good condition in just 70 feet of water. An intermediate to advanced dive, the site is home to many barracudas and large rays.

Tug Boat. Beginners as well as snorkelers enjoy the tug boat, beached in just 20 feet of water. The site is popular with many types of marine life, including jacks, grunts and even a ray or two.

Brassball **Wreck.** Another shallow-water wreck, the *Brassball* lies in just 25 feet of water, making it popular with beginners as well as snorkelers and underwater photographers.

Dive Operators

Dive operators on St. Kitts can provide instruction, rentals and transportation to surrounding dive sites. However, most island operators cannot provide a full range of photographic gear rentals and many do not accept credit cards. Check first.

Blue Water Safaris, ☎ 869-465-9838; **Kenneth's Dive Centre,** Frigate Bay Beach, Bird Rock and Newtown Bay Road, ☎ 869-465-2670 or 465-7043; **Ocean Terrace Inn Dive Centre,** Ocean Terrace Inn, Basseterre, ☎ 869-465-2754; **Pro-Divers,** Fisherman's Wharf and Turtle Beach, Fortlands, ☎ 869-465-3223; **St. Kitts Scuba,** Basseterre, ☎ 869-465-1189, fax 869-465-3696.

There is no hyperbaric chamber in St. Kitts or Nevis; however, there are chambers nearby in Puerto Rico and the US Virgin Islands.

Kayaking

St. Kitts has a new kayak route along the southern tip of the island. The 3½-hour trip is offered by **Turtle Tours** (☎ 869-465-9094) and no kayaking experience is needed. The package includes round-trip ground transportation, all equipment, use of double and single ocean kayaks, snorkel equipment and introductory snorkel lesson. The trip travels past the region's steep cliffs, often populated with mountain goats, vervet monkeys as well as cormorants, nesting pelicans and frigate birds. Visitors stop to snorkel along the reefs and get the opportunity to view an 18th-century shipwreck, a wooden vessel whose ruins were revealed by a recent hurricane. The cost is US $35 per person, children 6-11 are half price and children under six are free. Tours are conducted Tuesday through Saturday at 9 a.m. and 1:30 p.m.

Windsurfing

Tropical Surf on Turtle Beach (☎ 869-465-2380) has board rentals.

Fishing

Tuna, wahoo, dorado, kingfish, barracuda, shark and other game fish are found in the waters off St. Kitts. Fishing charter operators include: **Kenneth's Dive Centre**, Bay Road East, Basseterre, ☎ 869-465-2670 or 465-7043; **Ocean Terrace Inn Dive Centre**, Ocean Terrace Inn, Basseterre, ☎ 869-465-2754; **Tropical Tours**, ☎ 869-465-4039 or 465-4167; **Jeffers M.C. Enterprises**, ☎ 869-465-1900; **Sam Lake**, ☎ 869-465-8225.

Boating

Whether you want to go out on a day sail, a sunset cruise or a trip to a neighboring island, it's available from St. Kitts. We enjoyed a catamaran sail to Nevis aboard the *Spirit of St. Kitts*, part of the Leeward Island Charters fleet. It's a scenic ride from Basseterre to Nevis and comes with an open bar and a very friendly crew that's happy to point out sights such as the Southeast Peninsula and Booby Island, home to many of the island's feathered species.

Other offerings include: *Jazzie II* (glass-bottom boat), ☎ 869-465-3529; **Leeward Island Charters** (catamaran sailing), ☎ 869-465-7474; **Tropical Tours**, ☎ 869-465-4039 or 465-4167; **Kantours**, ☎ 869-465-2098 or 465-3128.

For those looking to man the helm, whether you'd like to learn to sail a Sunfish or happen to be an old salt that's ready to try your luck in competition, the St. Kitts and Nevis Boating Club has an activity for you. Every other month the club sponsors a day of fun with races, relays and lessons. For details and dates, contact the **St. Kitts and Nevis Boating Club**, P.O. Box 444, Basseterre, St. Kitts, West Indies or call ☎ 869-465-8035; fax 869-465-8236.

St. Kitts & Nevis

On Horseback

Equestrian lovers will find varied experiences on St. Kitts. Beginner, intermediate and advanced riders as well as children aged three and up can take a beach romp with **Trinity Stables,** ☎ 869-465-3226 or 465-1446; fax 869-465-9460. Headquartered near the Jack Tar Village, this operation takes guided rides on the Atlantic beach at your own pace for $20 US per hour. For $35 US, experience a three-hour-plus trip to the rainforest with a guide. Departures head up to the rainforest area by jeep then transfer to horseback for a guided ride through this lush forest.

Horseback riding near Jack Tar Resort.

Cultural Excursions

Plantation Safari

For a look at the plantation history of the island, visitors can take a full-day Plantation Safari with **Greg's Safaris,** ☎ 869-465-4121. The mostly off-road trip explores the windward coast plantations and includes the West Indian buffet at Rawlins Plantation. Learn more about the island's coffee, sugar and cotton industries on this guided trip.

Other Sports

Golf

 Two golf courses are found on St. Kitts. Test your skills at the **Golden Rock Golf Club** (☎ 869-465-8103), a nine-hole course near the airport. The Golden Rock Golf Club sponsors a day of fun on the last Sunday of every month. **The Royal St. Kitts Golf Course** (☎ 869-465-8339) in Frigate Bay adjacent to the Jack Tar was designed by five-time British Open Champion Peter Thompson. The 18-hole course stretches across the peninsula just beyond the all-inclusive resort. Fees range from $35-$40 for one or two players and use of the practice range is free.

Tennis

Tennis buffs will find courts at the **Jack Tar Village** near Frigate Bay. Day passes are available for non-guests; ☎ 869-465-8651. Two local clubs also invite guests: the **St. Kitts Bridge and Tennis Club** at Fortlands in Basseterre (☎ 869-465-2938); and the **St. Kitts Lawn Tennis Club**, Victoria Rd., Basseterre (☎ 869-465-2051).

Cricket

Watch the island's top sport at the **Leeward Islands Tournament**, which runs through May and June.

Basseterre waterfront.

Sightseeing

A day's worth of sightseeing is found on St. Kitts, more if you're especially interested in historic sites. Budget a day for an overall look at the sights, which range from historic homes and museums to natural formations and Indian petroglyphs.

The capital of St. Kitts and Nevis has had a rough time. Hurricanes, earthquakes, floods, fires, you name it, **Basseterre** has had it. Nonetheless, the city has come back each time and rebuilt. Today you'll find many historic sites in the city.

Circus, Basseterre. Yes, the circus is in town. This roundabout, modeled after Piccadilly Circus in London, is one of the most photographed sites on the island and is the heart of the city. In the center of the circus sits the **Berkeley Memorial Clock**, a popular meeting place. The green tower holds four clocks, one facing each direction and is named for the Honorable T.B.H. Berkeley, a local planter and politician.

St. George's Anglican Church, Basseterre. Just a short walk from The Circus is this building constructed in 1670, first named Notre

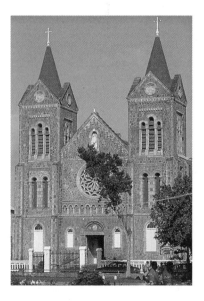

St. George's.

Dame. Burned by the British in 1706, the church was rebuilt, only to be destroyed by an earthquake and two more times by fire. The Kittitians are persistent folks, though and in 1869 they built the present church.

Nearby, a cemetery dates back as far as the early 1700s.

Independence Square, Basseterre. Stroll through this square near The Circus.

This historic site was built in 1790 and first used for slave auctions. It was renamed in 1983 to celebrate the independence of St. Kitts & Nevis from Great Britain.

Carib Beer Brewery, ☎ 869-465-8592. This plant offers a tour and complimentary tasting, by appointment only.

Petroglyphs, near Romney Manor. Don't miss the petroglyphs, carved many years ago by the Carib Indians. While you're stopped here, check out the handicrafts sold next door by a neighbor who creates turtles and bird feeders from coconut shells.

Carib petroglyphs near the manor.

Brimstone Hill Fortress National Park, ☎ 869-465-2609/6211. One of the top historical attractions in the Caribbean, make a visit to this fort whether you have an interest in history or not. From over 800 feet above sea level, you'll enjoy one of the best views found on any of the islands. On a clear day, you can view Nevis, Montserrat, Saba, St. Martin and St. Barts.

Brimstone Hill is nicknamed "The Gibraltar of the West Indies," and is one of the most amazing attractions in the Caribbean, a mandatory stop for anyone interested in military history. The structure took over a century to construct. It is made of volcanic stone and is named for the faint sulfur smell sometimes encountered here. At this site, the French and the British fought for control of the island, a battle first won by the French; the next year, the island was won back by the British.

Wear good walking shoes and bring along drinking water for your look at Brimstone Hill. (At the parking level, you'll find a small concession that sells water, soft drinks and snacks.) Your first stop

St. Kitts & Nevis

should probably be the brief film that gives an overview of the site and its rich history at the Visitors Orientation Centre.

From the parking level, walk up the cobbled path to the **citadel**. Here, a view of up to 70 miles makes neighboring islands seem just a stone's (or a cannonball's) throw away. From this lofty peak, it's easy to imagine the British forces keeping an eye on the seas over two centuries ago.

The citadel has two levels. Museums featuring Amerindian artifacts, British and French memorabilia and St. Kitts items are located in the stone rooms. Visitors can climb upstairs for additional views (watch young children up here, though; there are no railings).

The fort is open daily from 9:30 to 5:30. Admission is $5.

Brimstone Hill.

Southeast Peninsula. Once the last Kittitian frontier, this remote peninsula is now accessible by a modern highway. Some of St. Kitts most beautiful sights and beaches are located along this area, which is also home to many vervet monkeys. Turtle Beach is the most popular one on the peninsula (actually the only one where you might have a little company). On the drive, you'll pass a salt pond with a distinct pink hue, the result of many tiny krill shrimp. Birders will enjoy this region for its unspoiled opportunities to spot some of the island's species.

Caribelle Batik, Romney Manor, ☎ 869-465-6253. This stop is worth making even if you don't want to shop. Here, you can watch the batik-making progress and buy the finished product in the form of shirts, wraps and wall hangings or visit the ruins of the stately greathouse and the grounds shaded by trees that date back hundreds of years.) The closest thing that St. Kitts has to a botanical garden, these grounds are home to many tropical plant species. You can't miss the huge Saman tree, said to be the largest tree in the Caribbean. On the drive to Caribelle Batik, look for the historic aqueducts along the side of the road, a reminder of the island's early water system.

Where to Stay

 All hotels on St. Kitts charge a room tax of 7% as well as a service charge of 10%, so be sure to include them when calculating your budget.

Hotels & Resorts

Jack Tar Village St. Kitts Beach Resort and Casino, ☎ 800-999-9182, 869-465-8651; fax 869-465-1031. $-$$. Renovated after Hurricane Luis, this all-inclusive resort is recommended for vacationers looking for activity. Home of the country's only casino, the resort offers plenty of organized fun and evening entertainment as well as a golf course. The fun comes in an all-inclusive package, so all activities, along with food and drink, are included in the price. Although it is not located directly on the beach, it's just a short walk to the sand and surf. The cool, tile-floor rooms include air-conditioning, cable TV and telephone. As a clue to the resort's fun level, the pools are deemed the "quiet pool" and the "rowdy pool," where you might witness chugalug contests, bingo or pool volleyball. Other guest facilities include golf, tennis, bicycling, fishing in the lagoon, nightly entertainment, casino action, two restaurants and several bars, gift shop and duty-free shop.

Fort Thomas Hotel, Basseterre, ☎ 800-851-7818, 869-465-2695; fax 869-465-7518. $. Located within walking distance of downtown Basseterre, the Fort Thomas Hotel has recently refurbished guest rooms, as well as an Olympic-size swimming pool, one of the largest on the island. Facilities include a restaurant and bar, lawn and table tennis courts and beach shuttle.

St. Kitts & Nevis

Ocean Terrace Inn, Basseterre, ☎ 800-524-0512, 869-465-2754, fax 869-465-1057. $. This hotel combines the convenience of a downtown property with the relaxing feel of a resort. Just a short walk from Fisherman's Wharf Restaurant (a property under the same ownership), Ocean Terrace Inn or OTI, is a favorite with returnees to St. Kitts and with business travelers. The hotel has views of Basseterre Bay and Nevis; many of the recently renovated guest rooms overlook a pool with swim-up bar and a hot tub. Beautiful landscaping and walks made of stone divided with low-growing grass connect the hotel with two bars. Visitors can take a complimentary shuttle to Turtle Bay on the island's Southeast Peninsula for a day of watersports and beach fun, then enjoy an evening at the hotel listening to a solo guitarist in the Harbour View Restaurant or take in a show by the Coronets Steel Orchestra on Friday nights.

OTI offers special packages for adventure travelers. An Eco-Safari package includes seven nights accommodations, transfers, a half-day rainforest tour, historic sugar and coffee plantation tour, daily beach shuttle, sunset cruise and more for $605 per person (double occupancy). A Dive Package offers seven nights accommodations, two dives daily for five days, use of equipment, unlimited beach diving, sunset cruise and more; rates are $870 per person based on double occupancy.

 EARTH WATCH: *OTI has been instituting several eco-friendly projects. The hotel now buys recycled paper products; uses solar heating in 80% of the guest rooms; has a towel reuse program to cut back on laundry.*

Plantation Inns

If you're looking for peace and quiet, St. Kitts and Nevis's plantation inns offer good getaways and a chance to immerse yourself in more of the local atmosphere.

These small inns, built around historic greathouses on former plantations, are intimate properties that host only a handful of guests at a time. As part of just a small group, you'll get to know each other as you would aboard a small cruise. Often, the owners of the inn reside right on property, so you'll receive personal attention.

IS THIS WHAT YOU WANT?

Just as you would if booking a B&B in the US, ask plenty of questions before making your reservation at one of these establishments. These properties may offer limited services and may have certain restrictions. If applicable, be sure to ask:

◆ Is smoking permitted indoors?

◆ Are children allowed as guests?

◆ Is breakfast served at one time or as guests wander in?

◆ Are intimate tables available or are meals served family-style?

◆ Are special dietary considerations met?

◆ Is there a minimum stay?

◆ Does a remote location necessitate a rental car?

Rawlins Plantation, ☎ 800-346-5358, 869-465-6221; fax 869-465-4954. $$. As far back as 1690 a plantation now named Rawlins began producing sugar. At the time, the site was one of 50 or 60 estates that produced sugar on the island, using a sail-driven windmill to provide the power to grind the sugar. Nearly 300 years later, the greathouse, burned in a fire, was reconstructed and opened as an inn. Today Rawlins is in the hands of Cordon Bleu-trained chef Claire Rawson and her husband, Paul. The windmill remains as a reminder of that early history. Along with dining, the chief activity around here is pure relaxation. With no phones or televisions in the 10 guest rooms, the emphasis here is on leisure. The most romantic of the hideaway rooms is the honeymoon suite, housed in a 300-year-old sugar mill. Guests climb a winding stair from the downstairs living room to the upstairs bedroom perch, its walls made of volcanic stone. Facilities include grass tennis court, croquet, pool and crater and rainforest hikes. Breakfast and dinner is included in the plan as well as afternoon tea and laundry service.

Golden Lemon Inn and Villas, Dieppe Bay, ☎ 800-633-7411, 869-465-7260; fax 869-465-4019. $$-$$$. Fine dining and elegant accommodations lead travelers to the Golden Lemon, located on a black volcanic sand beach in the shadow of the island's volcano. One of the island's finest plantation inns, the Golden Lemon is owned and managed by former *House and Garden* decorating editor Arthur Leaman. The former New Yorker's sense of style shows in every room of the inn, from the open-air dining area where guests congregate to the immaculate guest rooms.

The property is composed of a 17th-century greathouse and 15 contemporary seaside villas, each filled with West Indian antiques and an atmosphere that invites relaxation. For the ultimate in luxury, suites offer plunge pools literally a step from the living room door. The hotel is located about 15 minutes from Basseterre and most guests rent cars for their stay.

Facilities include an excellent restaurant, tennis court and snorkeling on the offshore reef; no children under 18 years of age are accepted.

Ottley's Plantation Inn, ☎ 800-772-3039, 869-465-7234; fax 869-465-4760. $$. Legend has it that this 18th-century greathouse is haunted, but that doesn't stop the vacationers who come here looking for peace and quiet. Guest rooms in the greathouse and in nearby cottages are nestled on 35 acres of tropical grounds. Along with golf and tennis, guests can explore a small rainforest on the grounds and search for vervet monkeys. The inn includes a restaurant and swimming pool.

EARTH WATCH: *Even if you just stop by Ottley's for lunch, save time for a walk down the half-mile rainforest trail. You'll see lush forest growth, pass over a stone bridge and even have a chance at spotting the green vervet monkey (mornings and late afternoons are the best monkey-viewing times).*

White House, ☎ 800-223-1108, 869-465-8162, fax 869-465-8275. $$-$$$. Rates include breakfast, afternoon tea and dinner. With 90% European guests, the atmosphere at the White House is somewhat reserved and relaxing. The last greathouse built on St. Kitts, this inn offers unique guest rooms and a restaurant that's been featured in a national cooking show for its innovative cuisine. One of the guest rooms is set in a converted stable with wood plank floors, canopy bed, ceiling fan, stone wall and shuttered windows; other rooms might include twin sleigh beds with canopies. The great room is Caribbean elegant, with English furniture and a good selection of guidebooks to the local flora and fauna. Guests are served a full breakfast in this room.

Condos Horizon Villas Resort, ☎ 800-830-9069, 869-465-0584; fax 869-465-0785. $$. You'll feel as though you have made your home on this beautiful island during a stay in these lovely villas. Perched up on a hillside with a path down to a crescent-shaped beach, the villas are comfortable, cozy and maintained by a friendly staff. Guest facilities include a pool and a lovely little strip of beach.

Small Hotels

Bird Rock Beach Hotel, ☎ 800-621-1270 or 223-9815, 869-465-8914; fax 869-465-1675. $. Scuba divers especially enjoy Bird Rock, a property just five minutes from the airport or from Basseterre. The hotel is home of St. Kitts Scuba and divers can head right off the dock onto the dive boat. The hotel is simple and clean. Rooms include cable TV, air-conditioning, telephone and balcony or patio. There's a restaurant, dockside BBQ grill, pool, bars, tennis, fitness center and scuba.

Both scuba divers and snorkelers will enjoy Bird Rock Beach Hotel. There's good snorkeling just offshore along the rocks. Divers will find all levels of diving, including wreck dives. Offshore diving at the end of the 100-foot dock offers divers a chance to spot stingrays, eels and other marine life. The reef is found in just 25 feet of water and is good for beginners.

Where to Eat

A meal on St. Kitts means traditional Caribbean fare – snapper, grouper, salt fish or even flying fish – accompanied by side dishes such as breadfruit, pumpkin, yams and the obligatory rice and (pigeon) peas. Everything will be flavorful and often spicy. Wash down dinner with the local beer, Carib or the island's own liqueur: Cane Spirit Rothschild, or CSR. Made from cane, this clear liqueur was developed by France's Baron de Rothschild and is manufactured in Basseterre. A popular drink in St. Kitts is "Ting with a zing." Ting is a carbonated grapefruit drink sold throughout the Caribbean and, in St. Kitts, is mixed with CSR as an adult concoction.

St. Kitts & Nevis

Continental

Golden Lemon, ☎ 869-465-7260, $$-$$$. One of the island's best, this elegant restaurant takes over the patio of the Golden Lemon. A wide variety of dishes, fresh ingredients and an atmosphere that makes you feel like you're a guest in someone's beautiful tropical home make this a good choice.

Royal Palm Restaurant, Ottley's Plantation, ☎ 869-465-7234, $$-$$$. Dine poolside at the Royal Palm Restaurant, located across the lawn from the greathouse. Begin with an appetizer of conch fritters and move on to lobster quesadillas, shrimp ceviche or flying fish fillet for lunch. On the dinner menu you can enjoy pan-seared red snapper, herb infused tenderloin of prime beef or other favorites.

Rawlins Plantation, ☎ 869-465-6221, $$-$$$. Guests and non-guests stop by Rawlins Plantation for the daily West Indian lunch buffet, which features local favorites such as saffron rice, curried chicken and flying fish fritters, followed by soursop sorbet. The dishes are prepared using fresh seafood and herbs and vegetables from the Rawsons' garden.

Turtle Beach Bar and Grill, Southeast Peninsula at Turtle Beach, $. Located where the end of the island meets the sea, this laid-back bar and restaurant serves lunch daily and dinner on Saturday. Seafood and island barbecue are specialties. On Sunday afternoon, enjoy a buffet and sounds of the local steel band and anytime take in a great view of Nevis. Watersports, including ocean kayaking, windsurfing, sailing, scuba instruction and deep-sea fishing, are available nearby. You can pull on your mask and snorkel just offshore.

White House, ☎ 869-465-8162, $$$. This elegant open-air restaurant has been featured on cooking shows. Diners place their orders before the meal and enjoy a relaxing dinner in the open air dining area.

Caribbean

Fisherman's Wharf, Fortlands, Basseterre, ☎ 869-465-6623, $-$$. Relax in the informal seaside atmosphere at this open-air restaurant featuring local dishes. The restaurant sits on a wharf and offers romantic views of Basseterre at night. Live entertainment with local musicians and dancers make this a happening place.

Shopping

The best shopping stop is **St. Kitts' Caribelle Batik** at Romney Manor, where you can watch batik in progress. You'll hear an explanation of the step-by-step process and be able to buy the finished product in the form of shirts, wraps and wall hangings. Prices are reasonable and the batik makes a colorful souvenir of your island visit. We purchased a batik of a string band that brings back good memories of our island stays. (Even if you don't want to buy, it's worth visiting Romney Manor to see the grounds, which are some of the most beautiful in the Leeward Islands.)

In Basseterre, devotees will find plenty of selection at **Pelican Mall** on the waterfront. This two-story mall, designed with Kittitian architecture and tropical colors, features duty-free shops selling everything from china to liquor to Cuban cigars. Twenty-six shops make this a popular stop, especially for cruise ship passengers who come in from the new cruise ship berth adjacent.

Nightlife

St. Kitts is by no means a glitzy nightlife capital, but the island is home to a single **casino** at Jack Tar Village. The casino, open to adult island visitors, features slot machines, roulette, blackjack, craps, poker and mini baccarat.

St. Kitts & Nevis

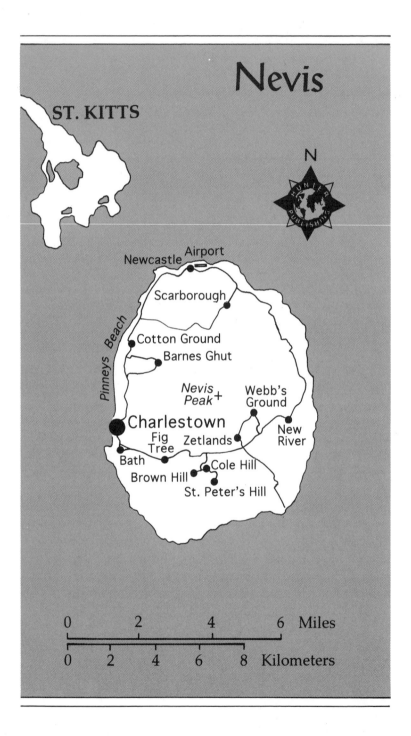

Nevis

Out on the Island

J ust minutes by prop plane and less than an hour by ferry from neighboring St. Kitts, Nevis is the quiet cousin in this two-island nation. The island was first named Oualie (pronounced Wally) by the Carib Indians, a word that means "land of beautiful water," an appropriate moniker. Today, the island's 9,000 residents are outnumbered two-to-one by wild vervet monkeys so nightlife on this charming isle often consists of watching raiding marauders sneak out from the lush cover of the bush and steal fruits on the hotel grounds. Nevis is especially favored by those travelers looking for a stay in a country inn. Both St. Kitts and Nevis boast one of the Caribbean's largest concentrations of plantation homes. The islands were once dotted with sugar plantations and greathouses, but today these stately mansions have been transformed into elegant inns especially popular with European vacationers and with Americans looking to experience a slice of the Caribbean "the way it used to be." Don't look for reggae lessons, limbo contests or mixology classes at these properties; instead, expect a sophisticated atmosphere where the emphasis lies, not on providing fun for its guests, but in pointing the way for independent travelers to make their own discoveries.

Nevis is one of the Caribbean's best destinations for the ecotourist. Rainforest hikes, birding, volcano hikes and plenty of flora and fauna make this island especially popular with nature lovers.

Getting around Nevis is a simple task – if all else fails, just stay on the main road and follow it all the way around the island to where you started. Most of the main road follows the coastline, skirting the steep slopes that lead to **Mt. Nevis.** From **Charlestown**, the road winds north adjacent to **Pinney's Beach**, one of the island's finest stretches of sand, and makes its way through the community of **Cotton Ground** and past the Four Seasons Nevis, the largest accommodation on the island. Past Cotton Ground, the road forks, following the coastal path to Newcastle Airport, Oualie Beach and

Nisbet Plantation, or taking the mountainous turn to Spring Hill, Fountain and Mt. Lily. Both roads meet up on the east side of the island and continue to traditional West Indian communities such as Brick Kiln, Whitehall and Mannings before turning back across the southem edge of the island. Here, the communities line the road, small villages with names like Chicken Stone, Pond Hill, Church Ground and Fig Tree. This region is also home to The Hermitage Inn and Montpelier Plantation, both in Figtree Parish.

Mount Nevis.

Getting Around

Rental Cars & Taxi Service

Rental cars are available on Nevis, but be advised that driving is on the **left** side of the road. A visitor's license is available from the Police Traffic Department for $30 EC ($11US). Excellent taxi and mini-bus service is available. The following chart offers sample rates from Newcastle Airport and from Charlestown. Add an additional 50% to hire a taxi between 10 pm and 6 am; add 20% extra to arrange a taxi after 6 pm.

TAXI RATES

Newcastle Airport to:

Charlestown	$11.00
Hermitage	$15.00
Golden Rock Estate	$15.00
Montpelier Plantation	$17.00
Nisbet Plantation Inn	$6.00
Mount Nevis Hotel	$7.50
Four Seasons Resort	$11.00

Charlestown to:

Nisbet Plantation Inn	$13.00
Golden Rock Estate	$11.00
Montpelier Plantation	$10.00
Newcastle Pottery	$14.00
Hermitage Plantation	$9.00
Mount Nevis Hotel	$14.00
Four Seasons	$6.00

Car Rental Companies

Car rentals, from small cars to jeeps, are available from several companies. Rental rates average about $40-$45 for a mid-size and $45 for a jeep.

Gajor's Car Rental	☎ 869-469-5367/1439
Nisbett's Car Rental	☎ 869-469-9211
Noel's Car Rental	☎ 869-469-5199
Parry's Car Rentals	☎ 869-469-5917
Skeete's Car Rental	☎ 869-469-9458
Stanley's Car Rental	☎ 869-469-1597
Striker's Car Rental	☎ 869-469-2654
TDC Rentals Ltd.	☎ 869-469-5690

Airport

Newcastle Airport is the port of entry for many Nevis visitors. The small airport is currently undergoing expansion so that it will be

St. Kitts & Nevis

;commodate larger aircraft. Currently, it is served by ute flights from St. Kitts.

Guided Tours

First-time visitors to Nevis would do well to take an island tour for an overview of the island. Although it is small, Nevis is home to many small villages and a guided look is the best way to learn more about the rich history of this destination. Guided tours are available from taxi drivers or from these tour companies:

All Seasons Streamline Tours, ☎ 869-469-1138; **Scarborough Tours,** ☎ 869-465-5429.

Beaches

 Nevis has several notable beaches, most of which are a toasted golden color.

Pinney's Beach. One of the island's best, the waters here are protected by reefs and popular with snorkelers, swimmers and sunbathers.

Oualie Beach. The most active beach on Nevis, with watersports operations.

Adventures

On Foot

Independent Hiking

Nevis is a hiker's dream. Walks of all difficulty levels are available both on a guided or a self-guided basis. The Nevis Historical and Conservation Society publishes a brochure called *A Hiking Guide to Nevis* that includes six hiking trails across the island; the brochure is available in the museums for $1. If you're considering a self-guided hike, invest in one of these brochures, which includes a map of the trails.

Each of these trails receives only minimal maintenance so hikers need to pack out all debris and strive to minimize habitat destruction.

If you will be hiking without a guide, advise your concierge or someone else at your hotel of your proposed route. They can tell you of any potential problems you might encounter (often the trails can quickly become overgrown due to tropical rains). Be sure to bring along plenty of water on any of these treks; you won't be passing concession facilities along the way. Socks and closed shoes are advised for all hikes.

The Source. This excursion takes about four hours round-trip from the Golden Rock Hotel. Maps are available at the hotel and lead hikers up to "the source" of Nevis's freshwater. The trail winds past a deep ravine, up through the rainforest and to a waterfall. Along the way, hikers have good views of St. Kitts. Be prepared to get muddy on what's often a slippery trail. The hike ends at a 120-foot ladder to the water source. Bathing in this area is forbidden and is punishable by fine because this is the freshwater supply for island use.

Round Hill or Telegraph Hill. From Mount Nevis Hotel and Beach Club, hikers can take off to the summit for views of Charlestown, Newcastle Airport and nearby St. Kitts. The hike takes at least half an hour and is considered moderately strenuous.

Golden Rock Nature Walk. The closest thing to a botanical garden on Nevis, this is a must-see for nature lovers. Head to Golden Rock Hotel and pick up a map (50¢) for a self-guided walk. The hike is easy but wear good walking shoes. Allow about half an hour.

Saddle Hill. Ruins of an old British fortress are found at this volcanic peak on the southern end of the island. From here, hikers have a view of both the Caribbean and Atlantic.

Nevis Peak. The most strenuous hike on Nevis, the peak can be reached by the Hamilton Trail or the Zetlands Trail (more difficult, although shorter). The hike takes about five hours and walks hikers through different ecosystems, starting at a dry evergreen forest and

St. Kitts & Nevis

working up to an elfin woodland. Rain jackets often come in handy on this hike (it is, after all, a rainforest).

Guided Hikes

For many travelers, guided hikes are the best option. These operators offer excursions that range from gentle walks to heart-pumping hikes.

Eco-Tours Nevis (☎ 869-469-2091) offers four walking tours.

◆ The **Eco-Ramble** is a 2½-hour hike covers the east coast of Nevis and travels to the 18th-century New River and Coconut Walk Estates to learn more about the diverse ecology of Nevis, view archaeological evidence of pre-Colombian Amerindian settlers and explore the remains of the last working sugar factory on the island. The hike is available Monday and Fridays at 9:30 a.m., Wednesdays at 3 p.m. and the cost is $20 per person.

◆ The **Sugar Trail Hike** looks at Montravers House, an abandoned greathouse. The easy 2½-hour walk goes into the tropical forest-covered slopes of Nevis Peak. It's offered Tuesday and Saturday at 10 a.m.; cost is $20 per person.

◆ The **Tower Hill Hike** travels past freshwater ponds and the ruins of a sugar mill before beginning the climb up Nevis Peak. The journey takes about 2½ hours and costs $20.

◆ **Historic Charlestown**. This 1½-hour walk begins at the birthplace of Alexander Hamilton, now the Museum of Nevis History and takes a look at this Victorian-era West Indian town. The tour is scheduled for Sunday afternoons at 3; cost is $10 per person.

Top to Bottom's Jim Johnson (☎ 869-469-9080) provides visitors with an enthusiastic look at the island's birds and plants. Some hikes offered by this operator include:

◆ **Green Ghaut Hike.** This vine-filled valley is verdant with flowers, ferns and philodendrons which are identified for participants. This is a challenging hike.

◆ **Jessups Reservoir Hike.** Climb into the rainforest to learn more about the plants, birds and insects on this moderately challenging hike.

- **Plantation Sunset Walk**. An easy walk, this route follows footpaths through an old estate to learn more about the island's botany as well as its history. Travelers see ruins, the oldest pond on Nevis and wild donkeys.

- **Starlight and Storytime**. This nighttime excursion looks at the stars seen in Nevis's clear skies and also listens to the sounds of Nevis at night. The evening ends with a beach campfire and the chance to roast coconuts and marshmallows.

Michael Herbert (☎ 869-469-2501) offers a half-hour hike to Herbert's Heights Nature Preserve, a gentle, sloping hillside. At 1,200 feet above sea level, it has the same panoramas as Nevis Peak, without the steep climb. This mountainside reserve is in the Rawlins area of the island and is especially notable for its rich flora and fauna, including mango, mammee apple and cocoa. At a bamboo orientation center, Michael leads visitors up a trail to the edge of the rainforest. A self-guided interpretive trail is also available with a lookout tower and covered picnic area with a telescope to view neighboring islands. The cost of the guided tour is $20.

Sunrise Tours (☎ 869-469-2758) has several guided hikes:

- **Nevis Village Walk**. This is a leisurely stroll through Charlestown for a look at traditional homes and stores. The two-hour walk costs $20 per person.

- **Saddle Hill (Nelson's Lookout) Hike**. The scenic hike follows trails that include views of St. Kitts, Redonda, Montserrat and Antigua. Guides point out medicinal plants along the way and you have a chance of glimpsing a vervet monkey. The three-hour hike costs $20.

- **Source Trail Hike**. This guided walk up to the source of Nevis's freshwater takes about three hours; cost is $30 per person.

- **Nevis Peak**. A challenging hike, this morning excursion to the top of the peak offers views of Montserrat, Saba, St. Kitts and Antigua.

St. Kitts & Nevis

On Wheels

Mountain Biking

 Mountain bikes are available from **Windsurfing Nevis** (☎ 800-682-5431 or 869-469-9682) for $20 per day or $120 per week. All bikes are equipped with safety helmet.

On Water

Scuba Diving

Nevis's sole scuba operator, **Scuba Safaris** (☎ 869-469-9518, fax 469-9619) is at Oualie Beach. Ellis Chaderton, a NAUI instructor and owner of the operation, reports that "Reefs here are in good shape. They're not overdone and are pretty much virgin territory." SCUBA Safaris, a PADI and NAUI affiliated operator, offers two 32-foot custom-built dive boats that can handle up to 14 divers each. Prices run $45 for a single-tank dive, $60 for a night dive. Resort courses are also available.

Chaderton notes that there are 40 dive sites in the Nevis vicinity, including coral gardens. Most wreck diving is done near Basseterre in St. Kitts. Night divers often see five or six turtles per dive. Visibility varies by location (visibility is sometimes poor on the south side of Nevis). Some top dive sites for Nevis vacationers include:

> **Monkey Shoals.** Two miles west of the Four Seasons Resort Nevis, this reef starts at 40 feet and offers dives of up to 100 feet in depth. Angelfish, turtles, nurse sharks, corals, sea fans, sponges and sea whips are noted here.

> **Booby Shoals.** This site, located off the coast of St. Kitts, is between Cow 'n Calf Rocks and Booby Island. It offers an abundance of marine life, including stingray, nurse sharks and lobster. This shallow site is up to 30 feet in depth and can be used by both certified and resort course divers.

> **The Devil's Caves.** Situated on the south tip of Nevis, this 40-foot dive has a series of coral grottos and underwater lava tubes. Lobsters, turtles, squirrelfish and needlefish are seen here by both certified and resort course divers.

Coral Garden. Two miles west of Pinney's Beach, this coral reef is home to schools of Atlantic spadefish and many large seafans. With a maximum depth of 70 feet, it's a favorite with both resort course and certified divers.

Champagne Garden. Just minutes from Pinney's Beach, this site is named for the bubbles created by an underwater sulfur vent. With its warm water temperatures, many tropical fish are drawn to this site.

Boating

A day spent sailing around Nevis can offer beautiful island vistas as well as snorkeling and swimming along secluded beaches. Call these operators to arrange an excursion:

Leeward Island Charters (catamaran sailing), ☎ 869-465-7474; **Nevis Watersports** (power boat rentals), ☎ 869-469-9690; **Sea Nevis Charter Boat Ltd.** (day sailing) Jones Estate, ☎ 869-469- 9239; **Newcastle Bay Marina Watersports Centre** (motor yacht), ☎ 869-469-9373 or 469-9395; **Sea Nevis**, ☎ 869-469-1997; **Nevis Water Sports**, Oualie Beach, ☎ 869-469-9690.

Catamaran trips are always popular.

Fishing

Deep-sea excursions are available from **Oualie Beach** (☎ 869-469-9735 or 800-682-5431).

Windsurfing

Windsurfers can learn basic skills on the bay at Oualie Beach. Advanced surfers can traverse The Narrows to St. Kitts, a two-mile passage that's often rough but a favorite with die-hard competitors. Or they can ride the waves and jump the reefs of Newcastle and Nisbet beaches. **Windsurfing Nevis** (☎ 869-469-9735 or 800-682-

5431) offers Bic and Mistral boards (race, slalom and wave) as well as lessons for any skill level. Rentals are $20 for the first hour and long-term rentals are available for $155 a week.

Equipment Rentals

Equipment rentals, including sea kayaks, boogie boards and sailboards, are available from **Oualie Beach** and the **Four Seasons Nevis** (☎ 869-469-1111).

In the Air

Day Trips

 A popular excursion for visitors spending a week or more on Nevis is to take a day trip to one of the neighboring islands. Many travelers make the quick hop by air to St. Kitts for a day of touring or hiking.

On Horseback

Ira Dore's Stable at Garner's Estate in the Newcastle area(sign up at your hotel activity desk) offers a combination trail and beach ride on Saturdays and Sundays. A horseman will even teach you English-style riding if needed. Rides last about 1½ hours and cost $40 per person.

The **Nevis Equestrian Centre** at Cole Hill (☎ 869-469-2638) offers guided tours of the Saddle Hill area, the historic plantations, Nelson's Lookout, historic Gingerland and other scenic points. Many of the trails offer good views of neighboring islands. Rides last about 1½ hours and cost $45 per person.

The Hermitage (☎ 869-469-3477) has an equestrian center and offers 1½-hour trail rides through historic Gingerland. Escorted trail rides are English-style and taken at the pace of the least skilled rider. Headgear is provided. For riders over 250 pounds, two Belgian horses are available. Three rides are offered: from Hermitage stable uphill to Zetland and Dunbar estates then to Old Manor and back to Cole Hill; from stables to Zetland, Old Manor, Stoney Ground and Golden Rock; from stable to the old Morgans estate of the Hamilton (cousin of Alexander Hamilton) and on to St. John Fig Tree church and Cole Hill.

Riding lessons are also available. And for those who'd rather let someone else take the reins, plantation carriage rides are offered. The relaxing two- or three-mile ride travels through historic Gingerland on hilly backroads where vacationers can witness traditional West Indian life. The carriages are authentic Creole adaptations of mid-19th-century Victorian styles and are constructed of West Indian mahogany.

Many horseback riding trips visit the Old Manor plantation ruins.

Eco-Travel

The Nevis Historical and Conservation Society (NHCS) works to conserve the island's natural resources. World Wildlife, USA awarded the society a grant to monitor six environmental study areas. The society works for environmental protection by publishing newsletters, supporting educational projects and sponsoring letters, media programs and visiting researchers. For more information on their environmental efforts, contact the **NHCS** at ☎ 869-469-5786 or fax 469-0274.

Cultural Excursions

Museums

The best source of information on Nevis's cultural history is the Nevis Historical and Conservation Society (NHCS). The society was founded in 1980 to conserve the natural and cultural history of Nevis by collecting artifacts and archival materials. Today, it operates two island museums: the **Museum of Nevis History** and the **Horatio Nelson Museum** (see *Sightseeing*, below). Along with the museums, the society works on environmental protection projects and architectural preservation.

In 1992, American Express awarded the NHCS a conservation award for the island's "Strategy to Preserve Historic Charlestown."

Other Sports

Tennis

The top tennis spot on the island is the **Four Seasons Nevis**, home to a Peter Burwash International tennis program. Professional coaches assist with lessons and competitions; many courts are lit for night play. Non-guests can play at the Four Seasons and also participate in round-robin tournaments. For more information, ☎ 869-469-1111.

Golf

Golf is a major draw at the **Four Seasons Nevis**. The resort is home to an 18-hole championship course designed by Robert Trent Jones II. Perched on a slope of Mt. Nevis, the course affords good views of neighboring St. Kitts. For information, contact the resort directly.

Gym

The island's only gym for general use is at **Oualie Beach Hotel** (☎ 869-469-9735). (The Four Seasons Nevis has a gym but it is for guest use only.) The newly constructed gym is available for a small day-use fee.

Sightseeing

Nevis' greatest asset is its natural beauty, a curtain of green lushness that envelopes Mount Nevis as it rises from the sea. Covered with a blanket of tall coconut palms, the hillsides invite slow drives and long walks. For most travelers, the greatest attractions are the island's eco-tourism activities, leisurely resort pace and golden beaches. Nearly all travelers spend a day, however, exploring some of the island's other charming sights.

It's worth a **walking tour of Charlestown** to enjoy the Caribbean architecture and historic homes. Once called "a sink of debauchery," today Charlestown is a sleepy little town that's proven to be a genuine survivor. Over the past 300 years, this city has weathered fires, earthquakes, hurricanes and warfare, but has kept its charming appeal, still seen in its Victorian-era West Indian buildings. Many of the early stone structures were destroyed by earthquakes in the 1800s. After that time residents began the practice of building first-floors made of stone and upper floors made of wood. Guided tours of this city are available from **Eco-Tours Nevis** (☎ 869-469-2091) and **Sunrise Tours** (☎ 869-469-2758).

Market Place, Charlestown. On Tuesday, Thursday and Saturday mornings, stop by the Market Place for a real slice of Caribbean life.

Baths Hotel and Spring House, Charlestown. Nevis island tours usually include a stop at the ruins of the Bath Hotel, built in 1778 for wealthy Nevisians to bask in 108° waters (until recently, modest facilities were open for visitors to "take the waters"). When it was built, the hotel was considered the most ambitious structure ever built in the West Indies. The waters, said to contain sulphur, ammonium and magnesium, were used by those seeking relief from arthritis and rheumatism. Five tile-lined booths offered a chance for a soak in the curative hot waters.

Museum of Nevis History, Charlestown, ☎ 869-469-5786. This small museum includes exhibits on indigenous people, Nevis' first residents approximately 4,000 years ago. Other displays include the island's political history, slavery, home crafts, churches and more. The museum is housed in the home that was the birthplace of Alexander Hamilton, first Secretary of the US Treasury. Exhibits recall the life of this famous Nevis resident. The museum is open Monday through Saturday. If you visit one of Nevis' museums, admission to the second (see *Horatio Nelson Museum*, below) is half-price. Admission is US $2 (children under 12, $1).

Bureau of Tourism, across from Dr. D.R. Walwyn Plaza, Charlestown. Stop by the Bureau of Tourism for brochures, maps and information on the island. The office is open Monday and Tuesday 8 to 4:30, Wednesday through Friday 8 to 4, Saturday 10 to 1 and Sundays whenever a cruise ship is in port.

Cruise Ship Terminal, Charlestown. Nevis' cruise ship terminal marks some of the newest construction on the island. The water-

St. Kitts & Nevis

front here sports a new face, with gazebos, benches and, soon, shopping.

Handicraft Cooperative, Charlestown. Near the Bureau of Tourism, this little shop is a must for arts and crafts shoppers and anyone looking to bring back a Nevisian souvenir. Look for wood carvings, small artwork and even Nevisian honey here.

Nelson Museum, next to Governor's House, Belle Vue, ☎ 860-469-0408. The name Horatio Nelson is heard throughout the Caribbean (see the Antigua chapter for more on this man) as a naval hero. The Englishman came to the region as an enforcer of England's Navigation Acts and was assigned to English Harbour, Antigua. In 1785 he came to Nevis. Two years later, the seaman married Nevisian widow Fanny Nisbet at a ceremony at Montpelier estate on March 11, 1787. Fanny Nisbet was given away by the future King of England, Prince William Henry (William IV). The captain went on to become England's greatest naval hero. The Admiral died at the battle of Trafalgar at the age of 47. Today his life is remembered at the Nelson Museum, the largest collection of Nelson memorabilia in the Western hemisphere. Paintings, china, figurines and remembrances of the naval leader are found here along with displays on Nevisian history. The finest museum in St. Kitts and Nevis, it is well worth a visit. The museum is run by the Nevis Historical and Conservation Society. Hours are Monday to Friday 9 - 4 and Saturday 10 -1. Admission is $2 for adults, $1 for children.

Saddle Hill and Nelson's Lookout. Located at 1,850 feet, this great stone fortress built around 1740 was once Horatio Nelson's lookout for enemy ships. Visitors have a good view of Redonda, Montserrat, St. Kitts and Saba from these heights.

Jewish Cemetery, Charlestown. Once a large population of Sephardic Jews called Nevis home (they comprised as much as 25% of the island's population), many coming to the island from Brazil. In the 17th century, the island was home to both a synagogue and a Jewish cemetery, with tombstones dating back to 1658. The cemetery is reached along a stone-walled path that's locally known as the "Jews' Walk" or "Jews' Alley." Nineteen tombstones mark gravesites at this cemetery.

Jewish Synagogue, Charlestown. The ruins of a Jewish synagogue dating back to 1688 are found just off the roadside in Charlestown. The site has been the location of several archaeological digs. Records in Amsterdam trace the building back to 1688, which would make it older than the Caribbean's official first synagogue in Curaçao that dates to 1732.

St. James Anglican Church, outskirts of Brick Kiln Village. Only two other churches in the Caribbean contain statuary of a black Jesus: one in Haiti and another in Trinidad. This historic church, still used by local residents for weekly services, is also notable for another unique feature. The church is also the burial place of former parishioners, with gravestones dating back to the late 1600s and early 1700s set into the flooring.

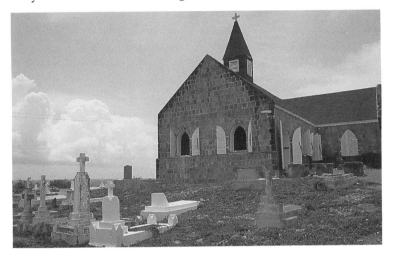

St. James Anglican Church.

Eden Brown Estate. Ready for a little ghost story? Time to make a stop at the Eden Brown Estate. These ruins, formerly an estate of a wealthy planter, were the site of a true tragedy. The legend goes that on the eve of his wedding a bridegroom planter and his best man got into a duel and both men were killed. The bride-to-be went mad and is said to haunt the ruins today. The site is grown over and is little more than a few stone walls, but for those with an active imagination it's an interesting stop.

Where to Stay

Hotels & Resorts

 Four Seasons Nevis, Pinney's Beach, ☎ 800-332-3442; in the US, ☎ 800-332-3442; in Canada, 869-469-1111; fax 869-469-1112. $$$. This is the most luxurious accommodation on Nevis and indeed one of the top resorts in the Caribbean. Boasting a championship golf course, 10 tennis courts, two outdoor Jacuzzis, 24-hour room service and more, this resort is for those who want a little pampering.

When word went out that the Four Seasons was coming to Nevis, doomsayers predicted the end of the quaint atmosphere for which Nevis is known. However, during the hotel's construction, Hurricane Hugo hit the island and the Four Seasons' bosses stopped building and put crews to work cleaning up the island. Today, the tiny island inns coexist peacefully with this corporate giant.

The Four Seasons Nevis sprawls across grounds dotted with coconut palms and other carefully tended flora. Guests can enjoy a round of golf, scuba, windsurf or just sun around the pool, cooled by Evian sprayed on guests by mindful pool attendants.

ECO-TOURS

The Four Seasons activities desk offers a large selection of eco-tours on both Nevis and St. Kitts. Ask to see the notebook detailing the tours and select from options that include history tours, rainforest hikes, horseback rides and even a starlight tour pointing out the constellations in the tropical sky, followed by a beach campfire to roast coconuts.

Mount Nevis Hotel and Beach Club, ☎ 800-75-NEVIS or 869-469-9373; fax 869-469-9375. $$. Those looking for a simpler accommodation will find some of the island's best views at this cozy hotel. This family-operated property sits high atop Round Hill Estate with a view of the Caribbean and of nearby St. Kitts. The view is best enjoyed from the open-air restaurant, well-known for its innovative cuisine. Rooms here offer a telephone, air-conditioning, cable TV and video players. The pool has a good view of the sea. The Mount Nevis Beach Club has a restaurant and beach pavilion. Independent travelers who would like to prepare some of their own meals will find a junior suite with kitchen available for $190 in the summer, $270 in the winter.

HIKES

From Mount Nevis Hotel and Beach Club, a one-hour hike up Round Hill to "Telegraph Tower" is available to hikers, both guests and non-guests alike. The peak, over 1,000 feet above sea level, affords good views of the island. Another popular hike is along nature trails that lead to Round Hill and Cat Ghaut Nature Trail, which winds among lady orchids, bamboo trees and, occasionally, some vervet monkeys. Even the hotel's grounds are of interest.

The property is on Round Hill Estate, a former citrus grove in the early 1800s. At the edge of the estate's lawn are the ruins of 200-year-old Cottle Church, built by Thomas Cottle, Nevis's president in the early 1800s. Early morning visitors to Cottle Church often encounter vervet monkeys or clouds of tiny white butterflies.

Oualie Beach Hotel, ☎ 800-682-5431, 869-469-9735; fax 869-469-9176. $. Watersports buffs will find one clear choice on Nevis: Oualie Beach Hotel. Home of Nevis's only dive shop and windsurfing operator, this hotel also offers a fine stretch of sand, 22 charming Caribbean bungalows with screened seaside porches and a comfortable atmosphere. Oualie (pronounced Wally) is the old Carib Indian name for Nevis and translates as "land of beautiful water." Oualie makes a good choice for families as well. Cribs are available, as is a kids' menu.

Windsurfing is available as part of a seven-night stay with five days unlimited windsurfing or a 14-day stay with 10 days of unlimited windsurfing. Scuba packages include two dives daily with the NAUI and PADI certified dive shop. Packages comprise a five-night stay with three days of diving or a nine-night stay with seven days of diving.

St. Kitts & Nevis

Rooms here are spacious and perfect for quick dashes to the beach. Four units include full kitchens. All rooms have a minibar, hairdryer, electronic safe, direct dial telephone, cable TV; air-conditioning is offered in the deluxe and studio units. Scuba, deep-sea fishing, windsurfing and sailing are available for guests and non-guests alike.

Plantation Inns

Golden Rock Estate, ☎ 800-223-9815, 869-469-3346; fax 869-469-2113. $$. This casually elegant inn is a favorite with eco-tourists because of the diligent efforts of its owner/manager, Pam Barry. A fifth-generation Nevisian, Barry emphasizes local culture, history and nature studies, offering her self-guided nature trails to both guests and non-guests. Her efforts have elevated this inn to one of the top Caribbean accommodations for nature lovers.

Tucked in a 96-acre preserve just steps from the thick forest, this inn features 14 rooms housed in seven charming cottages. A sugar mill dating back to 1815 offers a special accommodation for a lucky couple or family of four; the two-story room has two bedrooms (and some say a resident ghost). Public areas are housed in historic stone buildings. Most rooms are fairly simple, featuring locally made furniture.

But the real beauty of Golden Rock lies in its garden, where flowering plants and trees make this site beautiful. Early in the morning and late in the afternoon, vervet monkeys come from the surrounding rainforest and entertain guests with their antics.

Facilities include restaurant and bar, swimming pool, tennis, shuttle to beaches and beach restaurant. Special learning vacations emphasize history and culture or watercolor painting. Nature studies are offered periodically; call for details.

HIKES

Pick up a map of the Golden Rock Nature Trail and enjoy a 30-minute hike through the rainforest with a look at plants such as the flamboyant, screw pine, wild cherries, mahoe, mango, wild coffee and many more. Maps are also available for a four-hour hike beyond the nature trail to The Source, the site where Nevis' water supply originates. "We encourage people to go out and do eco-rambles," says Pam Barry. Both guests and non-guests are welcome to take a hike along Golden Rock's excellent nature trail. Donations are accepted for the upkeep of the trail; send them to Golden Rock Nature Trail, Golden Rock Hotel, Nevis.

For the best chance of spotting monkeys, come during early mornings and late afternoons around 4 p.m. Monkeys often congregate near the driveway, just behind the dining patio and along the walk. Pam Barry also offers guided excursions to observe the monkeys; ☎ 869-469-3346 for details.

Montpelier Plantation Inn, ☎ 800-223-9832, 869-469-3462; fax 869-469-2932. $$. (Children under 12 stay for $50 per night, under 5 years of age for $25 per night and under 2 years of age for $10. Children's rates apply only when the child shares the room with two adults.) Travelers may have heard of this classic plantation inn because of one of its most famous guests: Princess Diana. When Diana and her children visited Nevis, they opted for this hotel's quiet seclusion. Both royalty and honeymooners are offered peace and quiet in this very British hotel on the slopes of Mount Nevis. Princess Diana focused the eyes of the world on Montpelier, but it was hardly the property's first brush with royalty. On March 11, 1787 Admiral Horatio Nelson married Fanny Nisbet in front of a royal audience right on these grounds.

Today, the plantation includes a 16-room inn that exudes a dignified British air. The inn provides shuttle service to the beaches and evenings here are spent at the open-air restaurant that features classical cuisine with many local ingredients. The rooms are decorated in a tropical style and include telephone, ceiling fan, hairdryer, tea and coffee maker and patio; electricity is 220 volts with a 110 volt shaver adapter. Facilities include swimming pool, tennis court, restaurant and bar. The inn also has a private stretch of sand along Pinney's Beach with lounging facilities. Complimentary transportation to the beach is available daily. Montpelier closes annually from late August through early October.

St. Kitts & Nevis

ECO-RAMBLE & HISTORICAL NOTE

Enjoy an eco-ramble with Montpelier's resident industrial archaeologist to learn more about the history of Nevis. Also of interest to history buffs, Montpelier was the site of the marriage of Admiral Lord Nelson and Fanny Nisbet in 1787.

Nisbet Plantation Beach Club, ☎ 800-742-6008, 869-469-9325; fax 869-469-9864. $$$. (Children under 12 stay for $60 nightly; under 5 for $20 nightly. Children under 2 are free.) This plantation was the former home of Admiral Nelson's bride, Fanny Nisbet.

The plantation today is a 38-room inn boasting a striking quarter-mile palm-lined walk from the greathouse to one of Nevis's finest beaches. Guests stay in lemon-tinted bungalows scattered throughout the property. Today the greathouse of this former coconut plantation is home to an elegant restaurant and bar. There's a beach, pool and tennis courts.

The expansion of the Nevis airport into land near Nisbet has caused some concern for the peace and quiet enjoyed on the resort beach. Time will tell how much effect increased air traffic will have on Nisbet, which enjoys a peaceful atmosphere with an elegant clientele, many of whom travel from England for a two- or three-week respite during winter months.

Seven-night minimum stay is required for arrivals during peak Christmas holiday week.

HISTORY OF NISBET PLANTATION

On an island of fascinating historic properties, the story of Nisbet is perhaps one of the most captivating. Nisbet takes its name from Dr. Nisbet, the property's first owner. A keystone, found today in the ruins of the windmill in front of the great house, bears the date 1778 and the family initials. Frances "Fanny" Nisbet was the widow of the doctor and became the wife of Horatio Nelson in 1787. For years, Nisbet Estate was run as a sugar plantation and later as a coconut plantation.

Eventually, the property fell into the hands of Mary Pomeroy, daughter of one of the Knights of Malta. Fiesty Mary had an arranged marriage into another lofty Maltese family. One night, Pomeroy didn't like something her betrothed said from the other end of the table and threw a plate at him. Walking out, she never returned. During World War II, Mary was rumored to be a spy. After the war she moved to England to take up interior decorating. In the late 1940s, Mary Pomeroy's life took a drastic turn when a truck carrying steel girders lost part of its load, which fell on her. She was presumed dead and carried to the morgue, but she regained consciousness and demanded to be taken to the hospital. After two years of surgery, she came out with her insurance compensation (at the time, the highest ever awarded to anyone in England) and bought Nisbet in 1950. Mary eventually began converting rooms in the greathouse into guest accommodations; at the end of the decade she began adding cottages.

With the Anguilla rebellion in 1967, Mary was advised against returning to Nevis and struck a deal with Geoff Boon. He took possession of Nisbet and she took a property in Sint Maarten called Mary's Boon. Geoff Boon was killed in a flying accident in 1978 and Nisbet was purchased by three associates: George Barnum (who later sold the hotel to its present owner), Fred Kelsick (who died in 1988) and Bob Hitchins, the chief pilot of Carib Aviation (who died in a flying accident in 1987).

St. Kitts & Nevis

Hermitage Plantation Inn St. John, Fig Tree Parish, ☎ 800-742-4276, 869-469-3477; fax 869-469-2481. $$. The history of the island is the emphasis of this charming mountainside property which boasts such a classically Caribbean setting that it's often selected for fashion shoots. This plantation inn is built around a 245-year-old greathouse. Sprinkled around grounds bursting with tropical blooms stand restored plantation cottages that serve as the ultimate private guest rooms. Guests have access to a swimming pool and tennis courts, as well as romantic pursuits such as carriage rides and horseback riding. More room can be found in the luxury cottages, colonial buildings with separate bedrooms, antique-filled sitting rooms and full kitchens. All rooms include private porches with hammocks, four-poster canopy beds, mini-refrigerators, hair-dryers and ceiling fans.

The Hermitage.

Old Manor Estate and Hotel, ☎ 800-469-3445, 869-469-3445; fax 869-469-3388. $$. Plantation inn luxury as well as peace and quiet can be found at Old Manor. This 13-room plantation inn is custom-made for those looking to truly get away from it all. The atmosphere is quiet – really quiet – so book this inn only if you're happy with the sound of a braying donkey for your morning alarm (and with the occasional overheard conversations from nearby rooms). Rooms are large and bright, with white painted wood walls along with some stone interiors that recall the inn's previous life as a 17th-century sugar plantation. Both rooms and suites are available; select an upstairs unit for soaring ceilings and top views. Although baths are sorely in need of a facelift, the rooms are comfortable and romantically cozy. The grounds of Old Manor include ruins of a sugar works, now sprouting with local fauna and stone ruins that make a good spot to visualize a bygone era. On the foothills of Mt. Nevis, the inn offers free transportation to its beach facility, Beach-comber, on Pinney's Beach. Beachcomber serves an excellent lunch (and a good rum punch) and Pinney's Beach is one of the top stretches of sand on the island. Facilities include a swimming pool with great view of Mt. Nevis, whirlpool (not heated), restaurant and bar, beach bar and beach facilities and complimentary laundry service.

Small Inns

Hurricane Cove Bungalows, Oualie Beach, ☎ 869-469-9462; fax 869-469-9462. $-$$$. Independent travelers looking for the self-suf-ficiency of a housekeeping unit – as well as some of the most splendid views on the island – will love these stylish bungalows. Each of the 10 hill-hugging cottages was constructed in Scandina-via, broken down and reassembled on a slope overlooking St. Kitts in the distance. Today they're all open-air and furnished with Caribbean artwork. One- , two- and three-bedroom bungalows with kitchens are available and guests can walk down to the beach.

Camping

Call **Michael Herbert** (☎ 869-469-2501) for information about camping in the Herbert's Heights Nature Preserve.

Where to Eat

 A meal in Nevis means traditional Caribbean fare such as snapper, grouper, salt fish or even flying fish accompanied by side dishes such as breadfruit, pumpkin, yams and the obligatory rice and (pigeon) peas. Everything will be flavorful and often spicy. Wash down dinner with the local beer or liqueur.

Caribbean

Beachcomber, Pinneys Beach, ☎ 869-469-1192, $. This relaxed beach bar is open for lunch and dinner and features conch chowder, tannin fritters, a Nevis burger made of grilled mahi mahi or grilled fillet of wahoo. The atmosphere here is about as casual as you can get; order your meal then go take a quick dip in the sea if you like. Every Sunday the gift shop hosts a fun fashion show.

NO BUZZIN' HERE!

Visitors to the Beachcomber notice water-filled clear bags hanging from the eaves all around the perimeter of the restaurant. Bags are designed, say the management, to "reduce annoyance from food flies, sand flies and bar flies."

Continental

The Dining Room, Four Seasons Nevis, ☎ 869-469-1111, $$$. Although many lunchtime visitors to the Four Seasons Nevis select the open-air Grill Room, for a truly elegant meal they move to the greathouse's Dining Room. An elegant eatery where they can enjoy a candlelight meal, the Dining Room serves up many local seafood specialties accompanied by an extensive wine list. Entrées, such as saffron potato-crusted grouper with roma tomato and basil salad and snow peas, make this a special night out.

Montpelier Plantation, ☎ 869-469-3462, $$$. Evenings begin with a cocktail hour enjoyed in the great room as guests discuss their day while amiable owners James and Celia Gaskell take orders for dinner. Eventually, guests make their way to the verandah for an open-air dinner served with elegance and style. Some typical dishes include fillet of mahi mahi with a Swiss cheese crust, breast of duck in soy and ginger, tenderloin of veal and grilled lobster with Creole hollandaise.

Although many resorts make the claim, Montpelier is one that truly defines casual elegance and offers a taste of the Caribbean the way it used to be.

Mount Nevis Hotel and Beach Club, ☎ 869-469-9373, $$-$$$. This hillside hotel is well known for its reasonably priced contemporary accommodations, spectacular views and, most of all, gourmet dining. The Mount Nevis Restaurant, overlooking the aquamarine waters of the Caribbean and the sister island of St. Kitts, is highly regarded in gastronomic circles. Thanks to Chef Jeff DeBarbieri, this hilltop resort is now a dining stop both for guests and for day visitors. DeBarbieri, who trained with Swiss chef Gaspard Caloz at New York's Tavern on the Green, has created such specialties as lobster wontons with ginger-soy dipping sauce, grilled snapper with mango and tomatillo salsa and island spiced crème brûlée. "Nevis has tremendous fresh ingredients and a strong, interesting tradition of Creole cuisine," says DeBarbieri. "I try to blend these two assets to create memorable and appealing dishes."

Nisbet Plantation, ☎ 869-469-1111, $$$. The focal point of the resort is the greathouse, which dates back to the earliest days of the sugar plantation that began in 1778. This two-story greathouse, with a wide, screened verandah across the back, is a fine restaurant. Start your evening with a drink at the bar then step out on the verandah for a memorable meal accompanied by fine wine.

Oualie Beach Hotel, ☎ 869-469-9735, $$. This casual restaurant features the creations of Chef Patrick Fobert, who combines French recipes with a Caribbean flair. Diners select from chicken mousse filled with Creole conch, roasted rack of lamb in Jamaican jerk crust, tamarind rum-based wahoo loin and more. The panache of soup, combining pumpkin and secret ingredients, is a swirl of color not to be missed.

Shopping

 Stamp collectors will be familiar with Nevis because of its often-sought stamps. Stop by the **Philatelic Bureau** in Charlestown for the best selection. One of the best stops is **Nevis Pottery** in Newcastle, where artisans craft the local clay soil into various vessels. The pots are finished over a fire of coconut shells behind the shop. The shop is open Monday through Friday and is located near the Newcastle Airport.

St. Kitts & Nevis

Antigua & Barbuda

What's Special About Them?

The island of Antigua (pronounced an-TEE-ga) doesn't have the quaint shopping zones of islands like St. Martin or the lush tropical beauty of St. Kitts and Nevis.

What Antigua has are beaches: 365 of them, the tourism folks claim. Stretches of white sand that border turquoise waters teeming with marine life. Beaches where you can walk and hardly see another soul. Beaches where you can shop for local crafts and buy a burger at a beachside grill. And beaches where you can just curl up under a tall coconut palm and see the end of another Caribbean day, watching for the green flash as the sun sinks into the sea.

Antigua, which was battered by Hurricane Luis in 1995, is back to top condition. Some hotels were closed for refurbishments in the months following the storm, but most properties are up and running at full speed these days, sporting fresh facades and few indications that the island ever suffered such a terrible storm.

History

Pre-Colonial Antigua was originally inhabited by the Siboney ("stone people" in the Arawak language) Indians, whose hand-crafted shell and stone tools have been found at archaeological sites around the island. Some of these artifacts date back to 1775 B.C.

The next inhabitants of Antigua were the Arawak Indians, moving in about 35 AD and living here until about 1100 AD. These farmers were overthrown by the warlike Caribs, a people known for their cannibalism. The Caribs named the island Wadadli (today that's the name of the local beer).

In 1493 Christopher Columbus named the island in honor of Santa Maria de La Antigua of Seville, a saint at whose namesake church Columbus had prayed before his journey to the Americas. Even after European discovery, however, things stayed quiet here for a century, mostly due to the fierce Caribs and the island's lack of fresh water.

In 1632 an English party from St. Kitts landed on Antigua and claimed it for Britain, starting a relationship that endured nearly 350 years. In 1981, Antigua and Barbuda gained their full independence.

When European settlement began, Antigua was developed as a sugar-producing island and English Harbour became a home base for the British naval fleet. Admiral Horatio Nelson, Britain's greatest naval hero, directed his campaigns from the Dockyard at English Harbour.

In 1834, slavery was abolished and the sugar industry faltered. A century later, it was replaced by the tourism industry. In 1967, Antigua became the first of the Eastern Caribbean countries to attain internal self government as a State in association with Great Britain. Full independence was achieved on November 1, 1981.

TIMELINE

1775 B.C.	Occupation of island by Siboney Indians.
35 A.D.	Occupation of island by Arawak Indians.
1100	Overthrow of the island by Carib Indians.
1493	European discovery by Columbus.
1632	Antigua claimed for Great Britain.
1834	Slavery was abolished.
1967	Antigua attained internal self-government.
1981	Antigua achieved full independence.

Geography & Land

The island of Antigua is in the middle of the Leeward Islands, about 300 miles southeast of Puerto Rico or 1,300 miles southeast of Miami. The island is the largest of the Leewards, with 108 square miles.

Antigua is a limestone and coral island, somewhat scrubby with rolling hills, especially on the southern reaches. The highest point is **Boggy Peak** (1,330 feet). The capital city is **St. John's**, home of most of the tourist shopping and the cruise port. The south shore of the island is favored by yachties, who call into Nelson's Dockyard at **English Harbour**.

Barbuda lies 27 miles northeast of Antigua and covers 62 square miles. It's best known for its pink sand beaches. Redonda, an uninhabited island that forms the third piece of this nation, lies 20 miles to the west.

Climate

Temperatures range from an average of 76° F in January and February to 83° in August and September. Rainfall averages 40 inches annually.

Flora & Fauna

The national flower of Antigua and Barbuda is the **dagger log** (*Agave karatto*). A member of the lily family, this tall plant with dagger-like leaves can reach about 20 feet. It only blooms once in its lifetime and after the bloom the entire plant dies. The dagger log has been used for many purposes through the years, from fiber for robes to medicine for tuberculosis.

The national fruit is the **Antigua black pineapple** (*Ananas comosus*). The Arawak Indians first brought this fruit to the islands from South America.

Government & Economy

The two islands have a constitutional monarchy modeled after the British Parliamentary System. The head of the government is the Prime Minister. A bicameral legislature includes a lower House of Representatives with 17 elected members and an upper Senate with 17 appointed members. Elections are held at periods of no more than five years.

The economy of Antigua and Barbuda is heavily dependent upon tourism, but also includes some small industries and agriculture.

People & Culture

Most of the 67,000 population is of African descent with the remainder of British, Lebanese, Syrian and Portuguese origin.

Travel Information

When to Go

Just about anytime of the year means pleasant weather. The hottest months are during summer, when diminished trade winds make the temperatures seem even hotter. Prices vary throughout Antigua and Barbuda by season, as in the rest of the Caribbean. Here, however, high season extends through April to include the immensely popular Sailing Week. Look for accommodation prices to fall in early May and remain low through mid-December.

Cost

PRICE CHART

Dozen eggs	$2.30
Bread	$3.00
Bottle of rum	$6.50
Candy bar	$1.50

Customs

Passengers entering the country are allowed 200 cigarettes, one quart of liquor and six ounces of perfume duty-free.

Holidays

The hottest event of the year is **Antigua Sailing Week**, held in April. During this time, Antigua hotel rooms can be hard to come by. Nelson's Dockyard at English Harbour comes to life with the color and pageantry of the largest regatta in the Caribbean. Parties, barbecues, races, Lord Nelson's Ball and more highlight this annual event, now in its third decade. Other special events include the **Culinary Exposition** in May and **Independence Day** on November 1st.

Carnival is the hottest summer activity, scheduled in late July to commemorate emancipation. The events in-

Sailing Week attracts competitors from around the globe.

clude steel pan music, calypso, beauty pageants and parades with elaborately costumed musicians in bands of 75 to 300 members. Join in the fun and march with the musical troupes as they wind their way through St. John's. You'll find plenty of local food at Carnival City (otherwise known as the Antigua Recreation Grounds in St. John's): seasoned rice, *doucana* (a dumpling made of flour, sweet potatoes, coconut and sometimes raisins) and saltfish.

In late October and early November, the **Hot Air Balloon Festival** lights the skies. Close to a dozen hot air balloons schedule launches at English Harbour, Newfield, Jolly Harbour, St. John's, Curtain

Bluff and other sites around the island. To celebrate Antigua's independence, British sky divers jump from 2,000 feet carrying the Antiguan flag. Other festivities include parades, gun salutes and dancing in St. John's. A night flight over English Harbour makes for a spectacular scene.

CALENDAR OF EVENTS

◆ *January*

January 1, **New Year's Day** (public holiday), celebrated with windsurfing.
Antigua Winter Competition with course and slalom racing at Lord Nelson Beach.

◆ *February*

Antigua Grand Prix Regatta, Jolly Harbour.

◆ March

Good Friday (public holiday).
Easter Monday (public holiday).

◆ *April*

Antigua Sailing Week.
Cricket Test Match.
Department of Tourism Model Boat Race (pre-Sailing Week).
May 5, **Labour Day** (public holiday).
Curtain Bluff Hotel Pro-Am Tennis Classic.
Barbuda's Caribana.
Antigua & Barbuda Sports Fishing Tournament.
Whit Monday (public holiday).
Tourism Awareness Week.
Antigua and Barbuda Power Boat Race.

◆ *June*

International cricket.
Jolly Harbour to Barbuda Cruise and Race.
July 7, **Caricom Day** (public holiday). Carib Cup Regatta, Jolly Harbour.
Antigua Carnival Events and Public Holiday.
Antigua Open Class and Slalom Windsurfing.

◆ *August*
Antigua Carnival continues.
Antigua and Barbuda Football Tournament.

◆ *September*
Jolly Harbour Regatta (scheduled for last weekend).

◆ *October*
Annual Jazz Festival.
International Hot Air Balloon Festival.
Heritage (National Dress) Day.

◆ *November*
November 1, **Independence Day** (public holiday).
Antigua Open Golf Tournament.
International Hot Air Balloon Festival continues.
Carib Cup Regatta at Jolly Harbour.

◆ *December*
December 25, **Christmas Day** (public holiday).
December 26, **Boxing Day** (public holiday).

SPORTS CALENDAR: September-December is **basketball** season; December-July is **volleyball** season; January-July is **cricket** season; and August-February is the **football** (soccer) season.

Transportation

Most visitors arrive in Antigua at **V.C. Bird International Airport**, on the island's northeast corner. The airport is not only served by flights from the US and Europe, but is also a bustling hub for airlines such as LIAT for many inter-island flights.

FLYING TIMES: New York - 3½ hours; Miami - 2¼ hours; Toronto - 4½ hours; Dallas - 5½ hours; Los Angeles - 8½ hours.

Air service from North America is available from: **Air Canada**, ☎ 800-422-6232; **American Airlines**, ☎ 800-433-7300; **BWIA**, ☎ 800-JET-BWIA (US); **Continental Airlines**, ☎ 800-231-0856.

Antigua & Barbuda

Inter-island air service is available from: **LIAT,** ☎ 268-462-0700; **Air St. Kitts/Nevis,** ☎ 268-465-8571 (call collect); **Carib Aviation,** ☎ 268-462-3147.

US, Canadian and UK vacationers must show either a passport or a birth certificate and photo ID as well as an onward or return ticket. The departure tax is US $12.

Cruise Ship Terminal

Antigua is also a popular destination for many cruise ships. Two cruise terminals, approximately two miles apart, are located in downtown St. John's and are within walking distance of the main shopping areas. One is adjacent to Heritage Quay duty-free shopping center and the other is at Deep Water.

Private Boats

Private boats can enter Antigua through St. John's Harbour (west), English Harbour (south), the St. James' Club (south) or Crabbs Marina (northeast).

Special Concerns

Health

Doctors are on call at most island resorts and hotels and Antigua is home to a hospital. A recompression chamber is not available on the island but chambers are located in Saba and St. Thomas and can be reached by air ambulance.

Crime

Take the usual precautions you would exercise at home, especially on the larger and somewhat more congested Antigua.

Electricity

Dual voltage of 220 and 110 AC, 60 cycles is available in some hotels; converters from 220 to 110 are widely available.

Currency

The Eastern Caribbean Dollar (EC) is used throughout Antigua and Barbuda (as in the Leeward Islands of St. Kitts, Nevis and Anguilla). It is often referred to as the Bee Wee. The exchange rate is fixed at US$1-EC$2.68.

Tipping

Some establishments add a service charge to your bill; check first. A 10% tip is customary.

Marriage

Antigua is one of the simplest Caribbean islands on which to tie the knot. There is no waiting time, so you could fly in and get married that same afternoon. On weekdays, bring your paperwork (proof of citizenship and, if applicable, a certified divorce decree or death certificate of previous spouse) to the Ministry of Justice in St. John's, sign a declaration before the Marriage Coordinator and pay the $150 license fee. The Coordinator makes arrangements for a Marriage Officer to perform the civil ceremony. The Marriage Officer is also paid $50; payments can be made in US dollars.

Sources of Information

For materials on Antigua and Barbuda, including maps, brochures and rate sheets, contact the Antigua and Barbuda Department of Tourism closest to you:

In The US

Antigua & Barbuda Deparment of Tourism
25 S.E. 2nd Avenue, Suite 300
Miami, FL 33131
☎ 305-381-6762; fax 305-381-7908

Antigua & Barbuda Department of Tourism
610 Fifth Avenue, Suite 311
New York, NY 10020
☎ 212-541-4117 or (toll-free) 800-268-4227
Fax 212-757-1607

In Canada

Antigua & Barbuda Department of Tourism
60 St. Claire Avenue East, Suite 304
Toronto, Ontario
Canada M4T 1N5
☎ 416-961-3085; fax 416-961-7218

In Antigua

Antigua & Barbuda Department of Tourism
Long & Thames Streets
P.O. Box 363, St. John's
Antigua W.I.
☎ 268-462-0480; fax 268-462-2483

For more materials on hotels, condominiums and resorts, contact: the **Antigua Hotels & Tourists Association,** P.O. Box 454, Lower Redcliffe Street, St. John's, Antigua, W.I. ☎ 268-462-0374; fax 268-462-3702.

Another good source of information is the Internet Web page: http://www.interknowledge.com/antigua-barbuda.

Antigua

Out on the Island

The island of Antigua is shaped like an amoeba. Lined with numerous inlets and bays, the coastline skirts in and out around the island.

Unlike some of the Leeward Islands, which are circled by a coastal road, on Antigua roads radiate out from the capital city of **St. John's**, on the northwest coast.

Most travelers enter the island at **V.C. Bird International Airport**, on the island's northeast coast. Located about 15 to 20 minutes from St. John's, this end of the island is fairly dry and scrubby, with low rolling hills covered by low-growing vegetation.

North of St. John's lie **Dickenson** and **Runaway bays**, both popular tourist destinations and known for their excellent beaches. West of St. John's lies **Hawksbill Bay**, home of an excellent resort of the same name, with four picturesque beaches.

South of St. John's the roads fan out in various directions around the island. Various routes follow the coastline around **Green Castle Hill**; others take travelers to one of Antigua's top sites: **English Harbour**. Home of the historic Nelson's Dockyard National Park, this region is a favorite with eco-tourists and history buffs alike.

East of St. John's, roads travel to **Betty's Hope**, an old sugar plantation, and on to the island's most rugged shores. Here, the Atlantic waters meet the land, creating beautiful rugged vistas, choppy waters and several interesting geological formations.

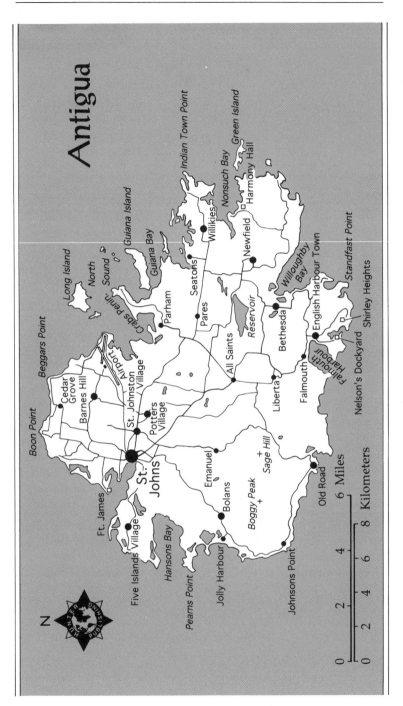

Getting Around

Car Rentals & Taxi Service

Taxi travel is the most common means of transportation, especially for travelers not comfortable with driving on the left side of the road. Taxi fares from the St. John's area to Nelson's Dockyard on the far side of the island run about $50 US, round-trip.

TAXI RATES

V.C. Bird Airport to Nelson's Dockyard	$21
Airport to Shirley Heights	$21
Airport to St. John's	$7

Car Rental Companies

If you want to see the island, it pays to invest in a rental car. You'll need to show a valid license (foreign or an international license) as well as a major credit card. Prices average about $40 to $50 per day.

A temporary Antiguan driver's license is required (US$12) and can be obtained at the airport or any Antiguan police station. We found that some roads are a little bumpy and that a full tank of gas (as well as a spare tire) was recommended for visitors traveling out on the island away from the major destinations.

Anjam Rent-A-Car	☎ 268-462-0959/2173
Hertz Rent-A-Car	☎ 268-462-4114/5
Avis Rent-A-Car	☎ 268-462-2840/7
J&L Rent-A-Car	☎ 268-461-7496
Jonas Rent-A-Car	☎ 268-462-3760
Budget Rent-A-Car	☎ 268-462-3009/3051
National Car Rental	☎ 268-462-2113
Romeo Car Rentals	☎ 268-462-3397
Richard's Rent-A-Car	☎ 268-462-0976
Dollar Rent-A-Car	☎ 268-462-0362/0123
Supa Rentals	☎ 268-462-7872

Antigua & Barbuda

Airport

Antigua's **V.C. Bird International Airport,** near the capital city of St. John's, is served by American Airlines, Continental and BWIA from the US and by Air Canada and BWIA from Canada. The airport is also a bustling hub for airlines such as LIAT for many inter-island flights. Small gift shops as well as limited dining are available in the terminal area.

Beaches

 The island's beaches are one of its strongest assets. All beaches are open to the public. Here are some top choices for a good beach walk, a day of sunning or just a little beachcombing:

Dickenson Bay and Runaway Bay. On the island's northwest side, these resort beaches are developed and offer plenty of fun.

Hawksbill Resort. Also on the island's northwest side, look for four beaches here, the last of which is clothing-optional.

Fort James. Northwest side. This beach is very popular with locals.

Galley Bay. On the Northwest Bay, this beach attracts surfers during the winter months when wave action is at a peak.

Rendezvous Bay. On the southern coast, this is a quiet beach for those seeking solitude.

Pigeon Point. Near English Harbour Town, this beach is convenient and a good place to cool off after a day of fun.

Half Moon Bay. On the southeast corner of the island, this beach is a national park.

Long Bay. Set on the east side of the island, Long Bay boasts calm waters protected by a reef and is a good choice for snorkelers and families.

LOOKING FOR THE GREEN FLASH

"Would you take our picture?"

It was another fresh-faced couple. Married maybe a few days, maybe a few hours. We'd had similar requests from two other duos as we sat on the sugar-white Antigua beach that evening. We were glad to oblige and perhaps a little flattered, too. Could they tell we were professional photographers? Probably not, although we did have a Nikon with us, somewhere in the beach bag. Then a sobering thought occurred – maybe we looked more like their parents than their fellow honeymooners. We grinned encouragingly as they posed arm-in-arm before a sapphire sea lit by the approaching evening. The young lovers smiled and the moment was frozen on film.

And we returned to the real reason we were on the beach this evening. Perched in a "love basket," a two-person swing/recliner that could symbolize couples-only resorts, we got in position for *the green flash.*

Not the superhero in tights. The lowercase green flash is a natural phenomenon often sought but seldom seen. Under the right conditions, as sunset cools into the sea, comes a momentary green sizzle on the horizon. Science explains it as the refraction of sunlight through the thick lens of the Earth's atmosphere. Island lore links it to romance: couples who witness the flash are guaranteed true love. All agree it's a rare sight, requiring just the right combination of sun, sky and luck. (Skeptics would add other requirements as well. "How many rum punches does it take to see it?")

Undeterred by such cynicism, we kept our vigil at the water's edge, like Linus in the pumpkin patch. It was a quest we had taken throughout the Caribbean, our Holy Grail of the islands. We had searched the sunset skies from the western edges of Jamaica, from sunset bars in Grand Cayman, even from the lofty heights of the Piton mountains in St. Lucia. No luck. Never even the slightest hint of a green flash.

But now, at Sandals Antigua, we couldn't help a mutual twinge of... what? Irritation that another sunset had almost come and gone and we had somehow missed the boat? All around, couples were celebrating their union, young Adams and Eves in a tropical paradise. We swirled the remains of our last rum concoction and admitted to ourselves that we were feeling more like inhabitants of Noah's Ark, herded two by two in this couples-only haven. The sun was dropping below a clear horizon. Only millimeters to go.

And then it happened. A green flash. "Did you see... was that?" After a decade of looking, could it be?

The instant of lime-colored light was undeniable, like copper coins igniting on our retinas. We turned to each other. You saw it? I saw it!

Soon we found ourselves walking hand-in-hand down the darkening beach. Ahh. Love.

A fresh-faced couple approached us and we smiled. Just one thing to do.

"Would you take our picture?" we asked them.

Adventures

On Foot

Walking & Hiking

Antigua has many hiking and walking opportunities. Walkers will enjoy a downtown stroll through **St. John's** as well as the national park at **Nelson's Dockyard**. For a challenge, hikers can climb **Monk's Hill, Boggy Peak, Fig Tree Drive** and **Megaliths at Greencastle**. Group hikes are sometimes arranged by the **Historical and Archaeological Society**, (fax only) 268-462-1469.

On Wheels

By Car or Jeep

For a scenic afternoon, **Fig Tree Drive** is a good one to enjoy in your rental car. It winds from the plains up volcanic hills of the Parish of St. Mary on island's southwest side. Fig Tree Hill is named, not for figs, but for bananas (which Antiguans call figs). Look for banana trees as well as groves of mango and coconut on this scenic drive. Off-road fun can be found at **Monk's Hill** for views from Great Fort George or Rendezvous Beach. Four-wheel-drive vehicles are available for rent from many operators.

Bicycle Rentals

Bicyclists will find 18-speed bikes for about $18 per day, $13 per day thereafter (or $85 for a week) from **Sun Cycles** (☎ 268-461-0324, ask for Errol Hodge). Five-speed bikes are also available. Free delivery and pickup from St. John's area hotels is included; there's a $10 delivery/pickup charge outside the St. John's area.

On Water

Scuba Diving

Antigua has a good variety of scuba sites: shallow reefs, deep coral canyons, caves and wrecks. Good visibility (from 50 to over 100 feet) and little or no current at most sites provides good diving conditions. The water temperature averages about 80°.

Some of Antigua's top scuba sites include:

The Chimney: Located southwest of Antigua, this dive features a small cave at a depth of 60 feet, with sponge-filled gullies descending to 80 feet. Look for large parrot fish, lobsters, eels and nurse sharks in the vicinity.

Thunderhead: Just a short boat ride from the west coast hotels, this site lies in 35 feet of water, making it popular with beginning divers. The wreck-strewn site features artifacts (medicine bottles and chamber pots have been found here) as well as hard corals.

Sunken Rock: Advanced divers appreciate this deep site, with a maximum depth of over 120 feet. The dive begins at 40 feet in a coral canyon that descends a sandy ledge. Divers then proceed down a drop-off to the bottom of the ocean. Barracuda, amberjack and rays are usually found here.

Dive Operators

Dive operators are found at **Galleon Beach Club,** ☎ 268-460-1024 (Aquanaut Diving Centers), **Royal Antiguan Resort,** ☎ 268-462-3733 (Aquanaut Diving Centers), **St. James Club,** ☎ 268-460-5000 (Aquanaut Diving Centers), **Rex Halcyon Cove** (Dive Antigua, ☎ 268-462-0256), **Runaway Beach Club** (Dive Runaway), **Jolly Beach Hotel** (Jolly Dive) and **Long Bay Hotel** (Long Bay Dive Shop, ☎ 268-463-2005). Certification is required and these operators offer lessons for full certification or resort courses.

Snorkeling

Look for good snorkeling at many sites around Antigua. We enjoyed snorkeling off **Hawksbill. Cades Reef**, an offshore site, is another favorite. If you'd like to experience a wreck dive without donning the gear, try snorkeling over the **wreck of the** *Andes*. This merchant ship sank in 1905 and can be seen in less than 30 feet of water. It is located in Deep Bay.

Windsurfing Antigua style.

Windsurfing

Constant northeast trade winds make this a good windsurfing destination. Beginners learn on the west coast, with its more protected waters, while the east coast challenges surfers of any level. The center of the windsurfing action is **Dickenson Bay**. Here the annual Windsurfing Antigua is scheduled.

Look for rentals at Buccaneer Cove, Dickenson Bay and Jolly Beach. Windsurfing lessons are offered at several hotels. Try **Club Antigua Windsurfing Sailing School,** ☎ 268-462-0061. The Lord Nelson Beach Hotel (☎ 268-462-3094) runs **Wadadli Windsurfing Classes**.

Deep-Sea Fishing

Grouper, snapper and other game fish are sought on deep-sea charters. These waters are the site of two tournaments every year: the Sports Fishing Tournament and the Winter Fishing Tournament.

The **Sports Fishing Tournament** offers over $50,000 in prizes. The angler who breaks the local blue marlin record (771.25 pounds, set in 1994) wins $10,000. Cash prizes also go to the record-breaking catches of white marlin, sailfish, kingfish, wahoo, dolphin and tuna.

The tournament donates part of its proceeds to a local cause or charity. Last year's event assisted the island of Montserrat, a member of the Leeward Islands that has been troubled by constant volcanic threat and is currently being evacuated.

About 70 boats participate in the event. Special fields include the largest fish caught by a female angler, the largest caught by a participant age 16 and younger and the most fish tagged and released by any one boat. The entry fee is $50 per angler for members, $70 for non-members and includes two days of fishing and admission and dinner at the presentation party. For information and an entry form, ☎ 268-462-1961.

Check with your hotel activity desk or with one of the charter boat companies for a day of sportfishing. Some operators are: *Legend* (☎ 268-462-0256), a 35-foot Hatteras sportfishing boat at Rex Halcyon Cove; *Lobster King* (☎ 268-462-4364), a 38-foot Bertram available for full- and half-day charters from Jolly Harbour; and *Overdraft* (☎ 268-462-0649), a 40-foot fiberglass fishing boat.

Sailing

Sailing is serious business on this island; many call Antigua the sailing capital of the Caribbean. April's annual Sailing Week attracts boaters from around the globe to English Harbour Town and is considered one of the world's top regattas. It's certainly the largest in the Caribbean and draws some of the globe's fastest yachts and top crews.

Sailing Week isn't all work and no play, however. The week is filled with parties, barbecues, road races and ends with a grand finale, Lord Nelson's Ball.

Whenever you visit, you can enjoy a leisure cruise, one that might include lunch, sightseeing, snorkeling and entertainment. Some fun cruises include: *Jolly Roger* **Pirate Cruise** (☎ 268-462-2064), Antigua's largest sailing ship, a two-masted schooner offering daily cruises; **Wadadli Cats** (☎ 268-462-2980), catamaran; and **Kokomo Cats** (☎ 268-462-7245), catamarans.

On Horseback

There are two options for equestrians on Antigua. **St. James Club** (☎ 268-460-5000) and **Spring Hill Riding Club** (☎ 268-460-2700) at Falmouth offer guided rides.

Eco-Travel

Birding

Birders will enjoy **Cobb's Cross Egret Colony**, in Nelson's Dockyard National Park on the island's southern coast. At sunrise, these egrets take off in flight, creating one of the best birding sights on the island. Nearby, the mangrove swamp at **Indian Creek** is home to herons, egrets, pelicans and the magnificent frigate bird.

Cultural Excursions

Field Trips

Learn about monthly field trips as a member of the **Historical and Archaeological Society**. This group publishes a quarterly newsletter on the society's many projects. For membership information, write Box 103, St. John's, Antigua West Indies. Fax (268) 462-1469 or e-mail museum@candw.ag.

Other Sports

Tennis

Tennis is a top sport in Antigua, with good courts found at hotels and private tennis clubs. May's **Antigua Tennis Week** is hosted at **Curtain Bluff Hotel**, a property that includes four championship courts, two lit for night play and a full-time pro. **St. James Club** has seven lighted all-weather tennis courts with a center court for tournaments. **Half Moon Bay Hotel** hosts three professional tennis tournaments: the **Men's International Tennis Championship** in January, the **Women's International Tennis Week** in April and a **Mixed Doubles Tennis Tournament** in October. Half Moon offers five all-weather Laykold tennis courts, a teaching pro and pro shop. **Temo Sports** (☎ 268-460-1781) is a tennis and squash complex with synthetic grass tennis courts lit for night play. Round-robin tennis tournaments are often scheduled and vacationers are welcome to join.

Squash

Temo Sports has two glass-back squash courts. **The Bucket Club** (☎ 268-462-3060) also offers squash facilities.

Golf

The most challenging course is **Cedar Valley Golf Club** (☎ 268-462-0161), an 18-hole, par-70 course. The course includes views of the north coast and is just three miles from St. John's. It was designed by the late Ralph Aldridge to fit the island's contour. In mid-March, the **Antigua Open** is played here by some of the Caribbean's top golfers. Fees are $20 for 18 holes, $15 for nine holes; carts are $25 for 18 holes, $15 for nine; equipment can be rented for $10 a day. A nine-hole course is available at **Half Moon Bay Hotel**.

Cricket

Cricket rules in Antigua. As much a cultural event as a sport, cricket was brought to Antigua by the merchants and military during colonial days. The season lasts from January to July and formal regional and international matches (called Test Matches) are held at the **Recreation Grounds** in St. John's.

Sightseeing

The capital of Antigua, **St. John's**, is home to about 35,000 residents and is the center of both business and tourist activity. Take a stroll around this historic city for a look at **St. John's Cathedral**, perched on a hilltop overlooking town, which was first constructed in 1682 and later replaced in 1789. It was rebuilt and reconsecrated in the 19th century after a devastating earthquake and includes two Baroque-style towers. Also have a walk by **Government House**, the official residence of the Governor General of Antigua and a good example of 17th-century colonial architecture.

Museum of Antigua and Barbuda, St. James. Located in the Old Courthouse, this museum includes exhibits of artifacts tracing the history of the islands from prehistoric times through independence.

Public Market, St. John's. This semi-open-air market is the place to go for local color and culture. Vendors sell their produce and locals stock up on fresh vegetables, spices and fish in this genuine Caribbean market.

Heritage Quay, St. John's. This shopping complex is just steps away from the cruise ship pier and is home to duty-free shops.

Redcliffe Quay, St. John's. Also a popular shopping district for vacationers, this restored arsenal houses shops as well as restaurants.

Nelson's Dockyard National Park, English Harbour. Built in 1784, this was the headquarters of Admiral Horatio Nelson, the commander of the Leeward Islands fleet. This site is a "must-see" on Antigua, even if you're not a maritime history buff. Make time to visit the Dow's Hill Interpretation Centre, with exhibits on history, culture and nature. "Reflections of the Sun" multimedia presentation traces the history of Antigua and Barbuda from prehistoric times to the present.

Copper and Lumber Store, English Harbour. The hotel was once a bustling center of marine activity near the docks. The bottom story served as a supply store and the upper floors were used as quarters for sailors whose ships were being hauled in for repairs. Today, those quarters are elegant rooms of a Georgian hotel and filled with period furnishings. Two other buildings, the old Capstan House and the Cordage and Canvas Store, have been restored for additional hotel space by the Copper and Lumber owners.

Admiral's House, English Harbour. The museum (just look for the bust of Nelson framed in the doorway) is an original structure and is filled with mementos of England's most famous naval commander.

Clarence House, English Harbour. This was once the home of Prince William Henry, duke of Clarence, who later became King William IV. The Georgian stone residence overlooks the dockyard and is now home to the Governor General. When he is not in residence, the home is open to the public with tours that discuss the house's origins and history.

Shirley Heights, Nelson's Dockyard National Park, English Harbour. To the north of English Harbour, these ruins were named for General Thomas Shirley, former Governor of the Leeward Islands. The fortress includes extensive fortifications, barracks and powder magazines which serve as good places to enjoy the view. On Sunday afternoons, Shirley Heights is a gathering spot where vacationers can enjoy local reggae and steel bands and traditional barbecue as they watch the sun set over the dockyard. Walkers and hikers can reach Shirley Heights on the Lookout Trail. This nature walk ascends from the harbor through a thicket of trees.

Fort Berkeley, English Harbour. About a 10-minute walk from the dockyard, these ruins were once a small outpost with eight cannons.

Betty's Hope Estate. This plantation introduced large-scale sugar cultivation and innovative methods of processing sugar to the island. It was founded in the 1650s by Governor Keynell and granted to Christopher Codrington in 1688. the Codrington family had interests in Betty's Hope for more than 250 years until 1920. Both Christopher Codrington and his son served as the Governor

General of the Leeward Islands. Today, two windmill towers stand along with walls and arches of the boiling house. A recently completed conservation project has refurbished this site.

Harmony Hall. One of the Caribbean's most noted art galleries, Harmony Hall features regularly scheduled exhibits and shows. The complex includes a greathouse, now home to a gift shop and galleries and a sugar mill, first restored in 1843, which offers a 360° lookout over the waters of Nonsuch Bay. These buildings were formerly part of the Montpelier Sugar Estate and today the complex also includes two guest cottages on six acres of land. Lunch is served daily at the Mill Bar and Restaurant (dinner on Thursday, Friday and Saturday evenings) with local fare. For more information, ☎ 268-460-4120.

Indian Town National Park. The island's eastern end is home to Indian Town Point, which may have been an old Arawak campsite. Look for the Devil's Bridge, a limestone arch on the seashore. Blowholes often form when the waves are at a peak.

Where to Stay

Accommodations in Antigua have a room tax of 8.5% and service charge of 10%.

Hotels & Resorts

Half Moon Bay Hotel, ☎ 800-9-953-3244, 268-460-4300; fax 268-460-3406. $$$. One of the Caribbean's most noted tennis destinations, this all-inclusive resort has not yet reopened following damage by Hurricane Luis.

Antigua Village, ☎ 800-447-7462, 268-462-2930. $-$$. Located at the edge of Dickenson Bay, this village is composed of Mediterranean-style villas on a one-mile stretch of sand. Studio, one- and two-bedroom apartments are available and include either a patio or balcony.

Hawksbill Resort, ☎ 800-223-6510, 268-462-0301, fax 268-462-1515. $$$. Just a few minutes from St. John's, this resort is our favorite kind: quiet, restful and nestled on not one, but four superb beaches. With a primarily British contingency, the resort is somewhat reserved but just a few minutes from the action of St. John's. The 37-acre property includes cottages and low-profile buildings that house 113 units. Nudists can wander over to the fourth beach to seek the total tan at the only nude beach in Antigua.

Sandals Antigua, ☎ 800-SANDALS, 268-462-0267. $$$. Like the other couples-only resorts in this popular chain, Sandals Antigua offers an array of activities that can keep even the most restless vacationer happy. Activity coordinators or Playmakers, keep things going for those who want to stay busy. For couples preferring inactivity, two-person hammocks and "love baskets," swinging wicker baskets, offer quiet afternoons beneath shady palapas.

A three-night minimum is required.

EARTH WATCH: *The Sandals properties have in place an elaborate system of environmental initiatives. "We must conserve the environment for two reasons," says owner Gordon "Butch" Stewart. "First, we depend on it for our livelihood – tourism – and, secondly, we owe it to future generations." Sandals' environmental program establishes water and energy conservation measures, including solar energy-heated water and innovative recycling efforts such as use of discarded copper pipes to create unique sculptures. Energy-saving light bulbs, environmentally friendly chemicals and in-house paper recycling are part of the resort's efforts. Every Sandals dive program includes an environmental education program focusing on protecting marine life and a "no picking, no touching" policy is enforced on all dive and snorkel trips.*

Curtain Bluff Hotel, ☎ 800-672-5833, 268-462-8400; fax 268-462-8409. $$$. This exclusive hotel, home of one of the Caribbean's best wine cellars, is located on a private peninsula with two beaches. The all-inclusive property includes all meals, drinks, afternoon tea, watersports, tennis, golf and even mail service so you can send those postcards home.

Galleon Beach Club, ☎ 800-223-9815. $$. Located in Antigua's National Park on the island's southern tip, this hotel offers one- and two-bedroom cottages and suites with fully equipped kitchens, living rooms and large sundecks, all overlooking the beaches at

Freeman's Bay and English Harbour. Complimentary amenities include daily maid service, fresh flowers, ferry service to the dockyard, watersports, tennis and beach chairs. Restaurant and bar on premises.

Club Antigua, ☎ 800-777-1250. $. Near St. John's, this all-inclusive property is a large one, with over 470 guest rooms. The all-inclusive package includes watersports such as Sunfish sailing, snorkeling, waterskiing and windsurfing. Eight tennis courts are on the hotel grounds (six lit for night play).

Condos Jolly Harbour Marina Club, ☎ 800-777-1250. $$$. Just 20 minutes outside St. John's, this 500-acre property has two-bedroom apartments with waterside patio, mooring space and full kitchen. The Jolly Harbour Marina offers more than 40 shops and restaurants. The beach is nearby and a freshwater pool is available at the sports complex.

Small Inns

The Admiral's Inn, ☎ 268-460-1027; fax 268-460-1534. $. Set right in Nelson's Dockyard, this 17th-century building now offers 14 guest rooms (each with two twin beds). The rooms are decorated with antiques, wrought-iron chandeliers and hand-hewn beams; some feature air-conditioning. The inn hosts the awards ceremonies for April's Sailing Week, so book very early during that peak time.

Camping

Antigua offers campers a unique option: escorted camping. **Katy-K Camp Excursion** meets participants at their hotel Monday, Wednesday or Friday at 1:30 for an excursion that starts with a nature boat cruise along the scenic Mangrove Harbors off Antigua's northeastern coast. After snorkeling, the group overnights on Bird Island, a mile off Antigua. "Besides setting up and maintaining campsites and preparing tasty meals, our experienced staff members are very knowledgeable naturalists and are enthusiastic about sharing their experience. Participants should bring along their curiosity and cameras," said Werner Meyer, captain of Katy-K. Campers have a chance of spotting stingrays, rock lobster, conch, over 50 species of tropical fish, leatherback sea turtles and the nearly extinct racer snake, actually a blindworm found on the reefs. Pelicans, frigate birds, white head wild pigeons, wild canaries and whistling ducks can be spotted overhead and on land five kinds of lizards can be identified. Fishing, nature walks, snorkeling and swimming are included along with meals and transportation to and from Antigua hotels. The total number of campers is limited to six, accompanied by three staff members. Rates are $160 per person for one night, $320 for two nights.

For reservations and information, contact Willa Meyer at **Kiskidee Travel and Tours**, St. John's, Antigua, ☎/fax 268-462-4802. Reservations may also be made through local travel agents.

Where to Eat

At the resort restaurants, you'll find familiar dishes on the menu as well as a few island specialties, such as christophine (a type of squash), pepperpot (a spicy stew), *afungi* (a pudding of cornmeal and okra) and *ducana* (a pudding made from grated sweet potato and coconut, sugar and spices and boiled in a banana leaf). Save a little room to finish off your meal with a taste of the sweet Antigua black pineapple. The most popular beer on the island is Wadadli, made locally.

Caribbean

Lookout Restaurant, Shirley Heights. $-$$. With views of Nelson's Dockyard, this restaurant serves up local specialties: spiny lobster soup, codfish balls, Antiguan pineapple and grilled lobster with lime butter. Steel bands entertain on Sunday afternoons.

Hemingways Veranda Bar and Restaurant, St. John's. $$. Near Heritage Quay, this informal, second-story restaurant is located in a West Indian-styled building constructed in the early 1800s. Start with a Hemingways' fruit punch or pineapple daiquiri then move on to an entrée of Caribbean seafood or steak.

Continental

Admiral's Inn, Nelson's Dockyard, ☎ 268-460-1027. $-$$. This inn is also home to a very popular eatery with outdoor dining near the yachts that come to this dockyard from around the Caribbean. Along with great people-watching, the restaurant also offers breakfast, lunch and dinner. Save time before dinner for a stop by the lounge area filled with yacht club flags.

Calypso Café, Redcliffe Street, St. John's, ☎ 268-462-1965. $. This café offers a variety of local dishes as well as Continental cuisine in a garden setting.

Redcliffe Tavern, Redcliffe Quay, St. John's. $-$$. Just steps from the shopping district of St. John's, this restaurant is housed in a former red brick warehouse that dates back to the 19th century. Enjoy quiche, sirloin steak, smoked salmon or seafood in a casual atmosphere.

Vienna Inn, Hodges Bay, (no phone). $-$$. Austrian food in Antigua? Why not? When you're ready for a break from island fare, stop by this eatery for Swiss schnitzel, veal filled with ham and cheese and topped with egg, Wiener schnitzel or veal schnitzel.

French

Chez Pascal, St. John's, ☎ 268-462-3232, $$$. Dine in the dining room or the garden at this fine restaurant located at Cross and Tanner Streets.

Le Bistro, Hodges Bay, ☎ 268-462-3881, $$-$$$. The island's first French restaurant, this eatery is known for its haute cuisine and includes local dishes such as medallions of fresh local lobster in basil, white wine and brandy sauce.

Seafood

Coconut Grove Beach Restaurant, Dickenson Bay, $-$$. Situated on the water's edge, this restaurant specializes in fresh lobster and local seafood. Open for breakfast, lunch and dinner daily.

Shopping

The primary shopping area on the island is in **St. John's**, near the cruise ship terminal. It's worth a two- or three-hour excursion to have a look at the goods offered in the small boutiques around the island. Along the waterfront you'll find the most tourist-oriented shopping, with duty-free wares such as fine jewelry, perfumes and liquor. Look for Gucci, Colombian Emeralds, Little Switzerland and other fine shops at **Heritage Quay**.

Shopping in St. John's.

Besides these pricey gift items, you'll also find a good selection of tropical prints and batik fabric sportswear (made on the island) sold in this area. **Caribelle Batik** has an excellent selection of shirts, skirts and shorts in tropical colors. Nearby, **Redcliffe Quay** is a more scenic place to shop and have a drink or some lunch. You won't see the duty-free shops of Heritage Quay here, but you will find plenty of cool shade, brick courtyards and restored buildings where you can shop for Caribbean items or enjoy a cold beer in a charming atmosphere. If you'd like to get away from the tourist center, take a walk up to **Market Street** for shops aimed at the local residents, including many fabric stores offering beautiful tropical prints.

Outside of St. John's, head to **Harmony Hall** in Brown's Bay Mill. This art gallery, which originated in Jamaica, features work by many Caribbean artists. Original works as well as prints and posters are for sale, accompanied by crafts, books and seasonings that capture the spice of the island.

Nightlife

 Casino gambling is a popular nighttime activity, with several gambling houses to choose from. The most popular is the **King's Casino** in St. John's. A popular nightspot is **Jaws**, with an indoor/outdoor dance floor and live entertainment. The kitchen stays open until midnight.

Barbuda

Out on the Island

Mention Barbuda and most people will recognize this tiny isle for one reason: Princess Diana. The seclusion and privacy this island was often sought by Diana and draws many famous celebrities.

But Barbuda is more than a jetsetters' hideaway, it's also a nature lovers' island. Accessible as a day trip from Antigua or as a vacation destination of its own, this small island is much less developed than its larger sister. Outside the lavish resorts, the island belongs to the wildlife, primarily the feathered variety. It's also noted for its spectacular beaches, long stretches of either pink or white sand that divide the sea from the land.

Along with birders and beach buffs, Barbuda also attracts vacationers looking for quiet fishing, golf, tennis, snorkeling, diving and beachcombing on its more rugged northeastern Atlantic coast.

History

Even when Antigua was a vital colony, Barbuda remained unsettled. In 1666 Britain established a colony, but it developed slowly. One of the first families was the Codringtons, given a land lease in 1680. The name Codrington remains important in Barbuda today.

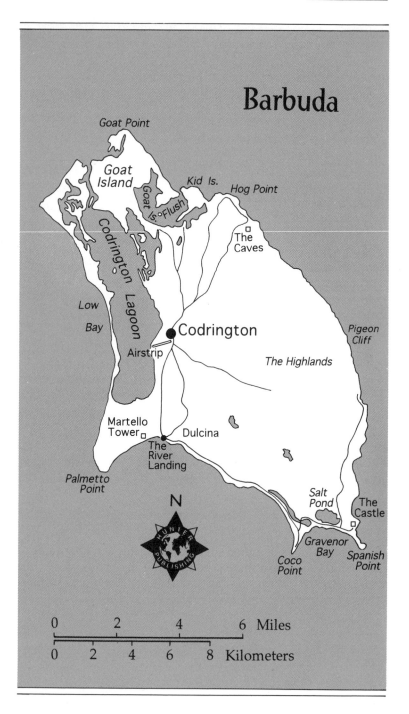

Barbuda

Goat Point

Goat Island

Goat Is.-Flush

Kid Is.

Hog Point

The Caves

Codrington Lagoon

Low Bay

● Codrington

Airstrip

The Highlands

Pigeon Cliff

Martello Tower □

Dulcina

The River Landing

Palmetto Point

N

Salt Pond

The Castle

Gravenor Bay

Coco Point

Spanish Point

| 0 | | 2 | | 4 | | 6 Miles |
| 0 | 2 | 4 | 6 | 8 Kilometers |

Getting Around

Taxi Service

Taxis are not just the best way to get around, they're about the only way. Don't look for rental cars on this island. Usually a taxi comes to meet the plane at every landing and can take you anywhere you'd like to go.

Guided Tours

Many of Barbuda's vacationers are day trippers from Antigua. Tour prices of $125 to $139 per person include round-trip air fare from Antigua, a sightseeing tour, a visit to the Frigate Bird Sanctuary and lunch. For information, ☎ 800-468-0482 or 800-981-8585.

Adventures

On Foot

Hiking

Barbuda is well known for its beaches, especially the pink beaches on the southwestern shore. The eastern shore beaches face the Atlantic and the waters here are rougher, but these beaches are best for beachcombing.

Walkers will find some good stretches along this windward side of the island. The eastern shore is home to the Highlands, steep cliffs that contain many caves, some carved with Amerindian petroglyphs.

Antigua & Barbuda

On Water

Wreck Diving

 Approximately 89 shipwrecks lie off the Barbuda shore, many of them not yet explored. It's excellent territory for scuba divers as well as snorkelers. However, if you're interested in diving off Barbuda, it is best to make arrangements at a dive shop on Antigua first. These operators can have your dive equipment sent by air or boat to Barbuda.

Eco-Travel

Birding

 Birders will find one of the Caribbean's top birding sites on tiny Barbuda. The **Frigate Bird Sanctuary**, located at the north end of Codrington Lagoon, is accessible only by boat and offers visitors the chance to view these imposing birds. The frigate bird (*Fregata Magnificens*) broods its eggs in mangrove bushes along this lagoon. With a seven-foot wingspan, this "man o'-war" can fly to 2,000 feet. It is avoided by other birds because it often slams into them to make them disgorge their food.

The frigate bird is easy to spot, especially the male. During mating season, which ranges from September to February, the male inflates a crimson pouch on his throat to attract the female. Chicks hatch from December to March and remain in the nest for up to eight months.

Other species often spotted include pelicans, warblers, snipes, ibis, herons, kingfishers, tropical mockingbirds, oyster catchers and cormorants. White-tailed deer, boar, donkeys and red-footed tortoises are sometimes spotted around the island as well as the famous Barbudian lobster.

Caving

Dark Cave is an underground cave with deep pools of clear water that extend approximately one mile underground. **Caves at Two Foot Bay** allows visitors to climb down into a circular chamber through a hole in the roof to view faded Arawak drawings on the walls. For directions and a local guide, check with your hotel. The **Darby Sink Cave** is another favorite, about 80 feet deep.

Other Sports

Golf

If you can't keep away from the course while on vacation, you're in luck. Golfers can try their luck at the **K-Club.** The club has its own nine-hole course.

Sightseeing

Besides animal- and birdwatching, Barbuda has several attractions. The ruins of **Martello Tower,** a beachside fortress, is one of the last of its kind in the Caribbean. This former lookout now affords some breathtaking views.

Spanish Point Tower (or The Castle) is another good lookout. Located on the island's southeast side, this tower was originally built to defend the island from the fierce Caribs.

Where to Stay

Accommodations on Barbuda have a room tax of 8.5% and service charge of 10%.

Hotels & Resorts

K Club, ☎ 800-223-6800. $$$. This is one of the Caribbean's most secluded resorts, the spot Princess Di used to visit to get away from it all. The resort includes 40 guest rooms on the beach with kitchenettes, gardens, showers and air-conditioning. Rates include all meals. The resort has a championship nine-hole golf course and two lighted tennis courts. The rates are ghastly, even by high

Caribbean standards. If you have to ask, you probably can't afford to stay here.

Small Inns

Coco Point Lodge, ☎ 212-986-1416, on island 268-462-3816. $$$. On the southern end of Barbuda lies this small resort. Its 32 rooms come with bath and beachfront patio. Small cottages offer kitchenettes. This resort is open only from December through May.

Booklist

Didcott, Charles and Christine. *St. Barth: French West Indies.* W.W. Norton & Co., 1997

Doyle, Chris. *Cruising Guide to the Leeward Islands, 1996-1997.* Cruising Guide Publications, 1995.

Eiman, William J. (ed.) *VIP Cruising Guide St. Maarten/St. Martin Area to Antigua and Barbuda.* Wescott Cove Publishing Co., 1992.

Gravette Andy G. *French Antilles.* Hippocrene Books, Inc., 1991.

Henderson, James. *The Northeastern Caribbean: The Leeward Islands* (Cadogan Island Studies). Cadogan Books, 1994.

Hubbard, Vince. *Swords Ships and Sugar : A History of Nevis to 1900.* Premiere Editions Intl., 1993.

Huber, Joyce & Jon. *Best Dives of the Caribbean.* Hunter Publishing, 1998.

Kincaid, Jamaica. *A Small Place.* Plume, 1989.

Luntta, Karl and Gina Wilson Birtcil (eds.) *Caribbean Handbook : The Virgin, Leeward and Windward Islands.* Moon Publications, 1995.

Rapp, Diane & Laura. *Cruising the Caribbean: A Guide to the Ports of Call.* Hunter Publishing, 1998.

Schnabel, Jerry and Susan L. Swygert. *Diving and Snorkeling Guide to St. Maarten, Saba and St. Eustatius.* Pisces Books, 1994.

Stone, Robert. *Day Hikes on St. Martin* (The Day Hikes Series). ICS Books, 1996.

Street, Donald M., Jr. *Street's Cruising Guide to the Eastern Caribbean: Anguilla to Dominica.* W. W. Norton & Co., 1993.

Index